Problem Solving Challenges

Don Miller
Bishnu Naraine

TRICON Publishing

Problem Solving Challenges

Transparency Masters
Related Problems
Extensions

Don Miller & Bishnu Naraine

St. Cloud State University

TRICON Publishing
Mt. Pleasant, Michigan

ISBN 1-883547-06-7

Introduction

The main goal of this book is to provide teachers with a ready source of non-routine problems designed to help their students become better problem solvers. In an attempt to accomplish this goal, the following problem solving strategies are introduced:

Look for a Pattern

Make a List

Solve a Simpler Problem

Draw a Diagram

Guess and Test

Use a Variable

Work Backward

Use a Model

The first section of the book consists of 32 pages designed to serve as overhead masters. The back side of each of these pages has a solution to the problem along with related problems and/or extensions. Answers to the **Related Problems and/or Extensions** follow each problem.

The eight strategies listed above are introduced in the first 16 pages. The purpose here is to provide students with specific examples that introduce and provide practice with these strategies. The other pages in section one (17-64) consist of mixed practice problems where the most appropriate starting strategy is not given. One way in which teachers can use this section is to start by presenting the overhead master to the entire class and then have students work in cooperative groups while trying to solve the problem. After allowing ample time for exploration of the problem, ask some of the groups to share their results with the class. Verbally trying to explain their approaches will help students better understand the problem, and consequently, will help them to become better problem solvers. **Remember** - before students will be able to reach the main goal, *finding a solution to a problem*, they will have to know how to get to the end result via problem solving **strategies.**

Section two starts by listing a strategy that can be used to solve the given problem. The purpose here is to provide students with additional practice in applying the strategies. The other pages in section two (73-114) consist of additional mixed practice problems where the most appropriate strategy is not given.

The problems in this book need not be used in the order presented. For use in the classroom, teachers should consider student backgrounds in selecting problems that may be appropriate either to introduce new strategies or to reinforce those previously discussed.

George Polya (1887-1985), the father of problem solving, devoted much of his life helping students to become better problem solvers. His suggested four-step process along with possible ways to implement each step are shown below.

1. **Understand the Problem**

   Restate the problem in your own words.
   What is given? What are you trying to find?
   Will making an estimate help?
   Have you previously solved a similar problem?
   Discuss the problem with a classmate.

2. **Devise a Plan (Strategy)**

Look for a Pattern	Make a List
Solve a Simpler Problem	Draw a Diagram
Guess and Test	Use a Variable
Work Backward	Use a Model

3. **Carry Out the Plan**

   Implement your plan. Does it lead to a solution? If not, go back and try to devise a new plan.

4. **Look Back**

   Is your answer reasonable?
   Does your answer satisfy all the conditions in the problem?
   Is there an easier or another way to solve the problem?
   Can the problem be extended to a more general case?

CONTENTS

SECTION ONE

SECTION TWO

Look for a Pattern

8	1
8	2
8	3
88	4
88	5
88	6
888	7
888	8
888	9
8888	10
8888	11
8888	12
·	·
·	·
·	·

1. How many 8's are there in the first 33 terms of the sequence?

2. How many 8's are there in the 77th term of the sequence?

3. What digit is in the thousands place in the sum of the first 21 numbers in the sequence?

8	1
8	2
8	3
88	4
88	5
88	6
888	7
888	8
888	9
8888	10
8888	11
8888	12
.	.
.	.
.	.

1. How many 8's are there in the first 33 terms of the sequence?

<u>Strategy: Look for a Pattern</u>

Terms	1-3	4-6	7-9	10-12	...	31-33
# of 8's	3	6	9	12	...	33

$3 + 6 + 9 + 12 + \ldots + 33 = \underline{198}$ (33 x 5 + 33)

2. How many 8's are there in the 77th term of the sequence?

The pattern suggests that the total number of 8's in terms 76, 77, and 78 is 78. Why? Hence, there are <u>26</u> eights in the 77th term of the sequence. Why?

3. What digit is in the thousands place in the sum of the first 21 numbers in the sequence?

One's digit: 21 x 8 = 168 → 8 ones + 16 tens

Tens digit: 18 x 8 + 16 = 160 → 0 tens + 16 hundreds

Hundreds digit: 15x8+16=136 → 6 hundreds+13 thousands

Thousands digit: 12 x 8 + 13 = 109 → <u>9 thousands</u> + . . .

RELATED PROBLEMS and/or EXTENSIONS

1. What is the sum of all the digits in the first sixty terms in the pattern of 8's? ($\underline{15,120}$ = 24 + 48 + 72 + . . . + 480 = 504 x 30)

2. A 10 11 12   B 14 15 16   C 18 19 20   D 22 23 24

   Use the pattern suggested above to help you find the missing terms:

   a. J — — —   b. — 98 — —   c. — — — 88
   (a. J <u>46</u> <u>47</u> <u>48</u>   b. <u>W</u> 98 <u>99</u> <u>100</u>   c. <u>T</u> <u>86</u> <u>87</u> 88)

3. Complete: 111^2 = _____ 1111^2 = _____ 11111^2 = _____
   What digit is in the thousands place of $11,111,111^2$? (<u>4</u>)

              PROBLEM SOLVING CHALLENGES

Make a List

How many different squares are there in the figure shown below?

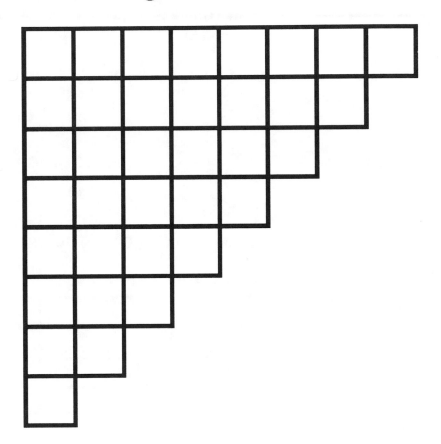

How many different squares are there in the figure shown below?

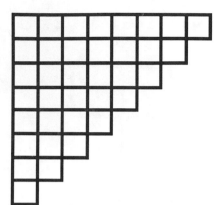

Strategy: Make an Organized List

Dimension	1x1	2x2	3x3	4x4
# of squares	36	21	10	3

Total # of squares = 36 + 21 + 10 + 3 = <u>70</u>

RELATED PROBLEMS and/or EXTENSIONS

1. How many different squares are there in the below figure?
   (<u>56</u> = 30 + 18 + 8)

2. I am thinking of three counting numbers which have a product of 48. Also, one less than twice their sum is a perfect square. What are my numbers? (<u>2</u>, <u>3</u>, <u>8</u>)

3. In how many ways can 22 be expressed as the sum of four odd counting numbers? Note that 1+3+7+11 and 1+7+3+11 are not different. (<u>18 ways</u>)

4. Kate has a collection of dimes and quarters worth $5.00. The total number of dimes in her collection is two less than four times the number of quarters. How many dimes and how many quarters are in her collection? (<u>30 dimes</u>   <u>8 quarters</u>)

PROBLEM SOLVING CHALLENGES

Solve a Simpler Problem

What is the arithmetic average of the first 99 numbers in the following set?

$$5 \quad 9 \quad 13 \quad 17 \quad 21 \quad 25 \quad \ldots$$

What is the sum of the first ten terms in the sequence of numbers shown below? The first N terms?

$$1/2 \quad 1/4 \quad 1/8 \quad 1/16 \quad 1/32 \quad \ldots$$

What is the arithmetic average of the first 99 numbers in the following set?
$$5 \quad 9 \quad 13 \quad 17 \quad 21 \quad 25 \ldots$$

Strategies: Solve a Simpler Problem Make a List Look for a Pattern

# of terms	1	2	3	4	...	N
Average	5	7	9	11	...	2N+3

The above pattern suggests that the average of N terms is 2N+3.
Hence, the average of the first 99 terms is <u>201</u>.

What is the sum of the first ten terms in the sequence of numbers shown below? The first N terms?
$$1/2 \qquad 1/4 \qquad 1/8 \qquad 1/16 \qquad 1/32 \ldots$$

Strategies: Solve a Simpler Problem Make a List Look for a Pattern

# of terms	1	2	3	4	...	10	...	N
Sum	1/2	3/4	7/8	15/16	...	<u>1023/1024</u>	...	$(2^n-1)/2^n$

The above pattern suggests that the sum of N terms is $(2^n - 1)/2^n$.
Hence, the sum of 10 terms is <u>1023/1024</u>.

RELATED PROBLEMS and/or EXTENSIONS

1. In the below sequence, what is the sum of:
   the first 99 terms? (99/100)   the first N terms? <u>N/(N+1)</u>
   $$1/2 \quad 1/6 \quad 1/12 \quad 1/20 \quad 1/30 \ldots$$

2. In the below sequence, what is the average of:
   the first 99 terms? <u>(204)</u>   the first N terms? <u>(2N+6)</u>
   $$8 \quad 12 \quad 16 \quad 20 \quad 24 \ldots$$

3. What is the ones digit in the answer for:
   4^{88}? <u>(6)</u> 7^{86}? <u>(9)</u>

4. Find the sum of the digits for each answer below:
   $111,111 \times 9,999,999$ <u>(63)</u> $22 \times 999,999,999$ <u>(81)</u> $999,999,997^2$ <u>(85)</u>

PROBLEM SOLVING CHALLENGES

Draw a Diagram

Of the 60 cars in a parking lot, 21 are neither two-door nor compact cars. There are 22 compact cars and 34 of the cars have four doors. How many of the two-door cars in the lot are not compact cars?

60 cars

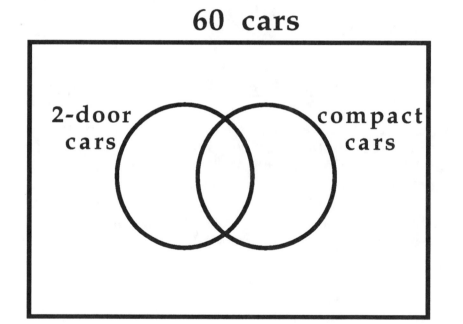

Of the 60 cars in a parking lot, 21 are neither two-door nor compact cars. There are 22 compact cars and 34 of the cars have four doors. How many of the two-door cars in the lot are not compact cars?

Strategy: Draw a Diagram

21 cars are neither 2-door nor compact cars and 34 cars are 4-door cars.
This implies that 13 cars must be 4-door compact cars. Why?

Therefore, there must be nine 2-door compacts. Why?

Hence, <u>17</u> of the 2-door cars in the lot are not compact cars. Why?

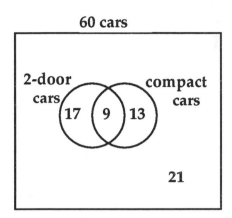

RELATED PROBLEMS and/or EXTENSIONS

1. A survey of 50 students at Discovery Middle School asked the following three questions: Do you like Science? Do you like English? Do you like Math? The results of the survey showed that:

   24 do not like Science   21 do not like Math
   14 like both Math and English   13 like both Science and English
   17 like both Math and Science   20 like English
   5 like English and Science but not Math

   How many students in the survey:
   a. like Science only? (<u>4</u>)
   b. like only Math and English? (<u>6</u>)
   c. like Math, Science, and English? (<u>8</u>)
   d. do not like any of these subjects? (<u>11</u>)

2. Of the 750 students enrolled at North Jr. High,
   • 3 out of every 5 students are enrolled in an Art class
   • 2 out of every 5 students are girls.

   How many boys at North Jr. High are not taking an Art class? (<u>180</u>)

 PROBLEM SOLVING CHALLENGES

Guess and Test

I am thinking of 3 different counting numbers. The smallest is 2 less than half the largest, the average of the 3 numbers is 16, and one is a two-digit prime. What are the numbers?

I am thinking of 3 different counting numbers.
The smallest is 2 less than half the largest, the
average of the 3 numbers is 16, and one is a
two-digit prime. What are the numbers?

Strategies: Guess and Test Make a List

Average = 16 $\Rightarrow$ Sum = 48

Largest # (X)	Middle #	Smallest # (X/2 - 2)	
30	5 (48-30-13)	13 (30/2-2)	No! (13 not the smallest #)
18	23 (48-18-7)	7	No! (18 not the largest #)
• • •			
22	17 (48-22-9)	9	Yes! (22, 17, 9)

9 < 17 < 22   (9 + 17 + 22)/3 = 48/3 = 16   17 is a 2-digit prime number

---

RELATED PROBLEMS and/or EXTENSIONS

1. Use all the clues below to help you find my three numbers.
   - All are different 2-digit counting numbers
   - The smallest number is 4 less than half the largest
   - The average of the three numbers is 21
   - One of the numbers is a prime number. (12, 19, 32)

2. Determine the number of different ways that 12 dimes can be placed
   into 3 boxes A, B, and C given that:
   - Each box must end up with at least 20 cents;
   - Box B ends up with more dimes than box A, and
   - Box B ends up with less dimes than box C.

   3 ways: | A | B | C | | A | B | C | | A | B | C |
   | 2 | 3 | 7 | | 2 | 4 | 6 | | 3 | 4 | 5 |

3. Find the difference between the largest 5-digit perfect square and the
   smallest 5-digit perfect cube. (99856 - 10648 = 89208)

Use a Variable

After the first two terms in the following sequences, each number is the sum of the preceding two numbers. Find the missing numbers.

Example: 1   1   2   3   5   8   13

a.   1 __ __ __ __ __ 53

b.   4 __ __ __ __ __ 4

c. __ __ __ 11 __ __ 50

After the first two terms in the following sequences, each number is the sum of the preceding two numbers. Find the missing numbers.

<u>Strategies: Use a Variable   Guess and Test</u>

Example: 1   1   2   3   5   8   13

a. 1 $\underline{6}$ $\underline{7}$ $\underline{13}$ $\underline{20}$ $\underline{33}$ 53

 x x+1 2x+1 3x+2 5x+3 8x+5 = 53

 x = 6

b. 4 $\underline{-2}$ $\underline{2}$ $\underline{0}$ $\underline{2}$ $\underline{2}$ 4

 x x+4 2x+4 3x+8 5x+12 8x+20 = 4

 x = -2

c. $\underline{6}$ $\underline{2.5}$ $\underline{8.5}$ 11 $\underline{19.5}$ $\underline{30.5}$ 50

 x x+11 2x+11 = 50

 x = 19.5

RELATED PROBLEMS and/or EXTENSIONS

1. After the first three terms in the following sequences, each number is the sum of the preceding three numbers. Find the missing numbers.

   a. 0 —— 1 5 10 —— —— 57 <u>(0 4 1 5 10 16 31 57)</u>

   b. 1 —— —— 2 3 —— —— 20 <u>(1 0 1 2 3 6 11 20)</u>

2. After the first four terms in the following sequences, each number is the sum of the preceding four numbers. Find the missing numbers.

   a. 1 1 1 —— 4 —— —— —— 49 <u>(1 1 1 1 4 7 13 25 49)</u>

   b. 2 —— 2 —— 8 14 27 —— 101 <u>(2 1 2 3 8 14 27 52 101)</u>

   c. —— 8 3 7 —— —— —— 93 179 <u>(-8 8 3 7 10 28 48 93 179)</u>

   d. 0 1 —— —— 2 4 7 —— —— 51 <u>(0 1 0.5 0.5 2 4 7 13.5 26.5 51)</u>

      PROBLEM SOLVING CHALLENGES

Work Backward

Carlos bought a bag of jellybeans. After giving his sister one more than half the beans, he ate 15. His brother then ate half of the remaining beans, after which there were 9 left. How many jellybeans were in the bag before it was opened?

Carlos bought a bag of jellybeans. After giving his sister one more than half the beans, he ate 15. His brother then ate half of the remaining beans, after which there were 9 left. How many jellybeans were in the bag before it was opened?

Solution I Strategy: Work Backward

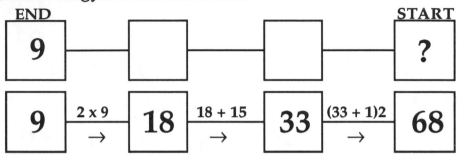

The above figure represents a solution to the problem. Try to explain each step as you work backward from the end result. There were <u>68</u> jellybeans in the bag.

Solution II Strategy: Use a Variable

Let J = # of jellybeans in bag before it was opened.

Gave	Left with
Sister $\to$ J/2+1	J - (J/2 + 1) = J/2 - 1
Himself $\to$ 15	(J/2 - 1) - 15 = J/2 - 16
Brother $\to$ 1/2(J/2-16)	(J/2-16) - 1/2(J/2-16) = 9 $\Rightarrow$ J = <u>68</u>

There were <u>68</u> jellybeans in the bag.

RELATED PROBLEMS and/or EXTENSIONS

1. Calvin's scores on three 50-point tests were 47, 44, and 39. What is the least possible number of points he must get on a 100-point final test to end up with an average of:

    90%? (<u>95</u>)   80%? (<u>70</u>)   70%? (<u>45</u>)

2. Four women have just finished playing 4 games. There was one loser per game. After each game, the loser was required to double the money that the other three had at that time. If all the players ended up with $80 and each lost one game, how much money did each of the two winning players make? (<u>$35</u> and <u>$55</u>)

           PROBLEM SOLVING CHALLENGES

Use a Model

Suppose an open top rectangular box of height 10 cm and base 16 cm by 24 cm is completely filled with identical cubes of volume 8 cubic centimeters. How many of the cubes touch either a side or the bottom of the box?

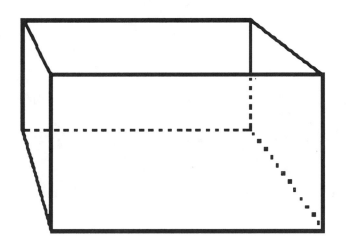

Suppose an open top rectangular box of height 10 cm and base 16 cm x 24 cm is completely filled with identical cubes of volume 8 cubic centimeters. How many of the cubes touch either a side or the bottom of the box?

Strategy: Use a Model

The edge of each cube is 2 cm. Therefore, the box holds 480 cubes of this size. Verify.

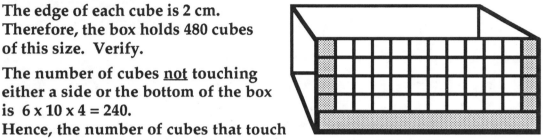

The number of cubes not touching either a side or the bottom of the box is 6 x 10 x 4 = 240.

Hence, the number of cubes that touch either a side or the bottom of the box must be **240**. (480 - 240)

RELATED PROBLEMS and/or EXTENSIONS

1. The surface of a cube is painted red. The cube is then cut into equal sized smaller cubes, 72 of which have two red faces. How many of the smaller cubes have:
   one red face? (**216** = 6x36)   no red faces? (**216** = 6x6x6)

2. An NxNxN cube is painted red and then cut into smaller 1x1x1 cubes. How many of the smaller cubes are painted red on:
      3 faces? (**8** corner cubes)   2 faces?   **12(N-2)**
      1 face?   **6(N-2)(N-2)**   No faces?   **(N-2)³**

3. Suppose an open top cubical box of volume 1728 cm³ is completely filled with identical cubes, each of which has a surface area of 54 cm². How many cubes touch either a side or the bottom of the box? (**52**)

99 Dimes

In how many different ways can 99 dimes be placed into two boxes so that each box contains at least $2.00?

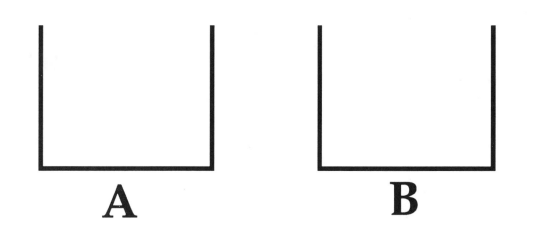

In how many different ways can 99 dimes be placed into two boxes so that each box contains at least $2.00?

A   B

Solution I Strategy: Make an Organized List

Each box must contain at least 20 dimes. Why?

# of dimes in A	20	21	22	23	...	78	79
# of dimes in B	79	78	77	76	...	21	20

The list suggests that there are <u>60</u> (79 - 19) different ways to place the 99 dimes into the two boxes.

Solution II Strategies: Solve a Simpler Problem   Make a List
Look for a Pattern

Each box must contain at least 20 dimes. Why?

# of dimes in A	40	41	42	43	...	99
# of ways	1	2	3	4	...	?

The list suggests that there are <u>60</u> (99 - 39) different ways to place the 99 dimes into the two boxes.

RELATED PROBLEMS and/or EXTENSIONS

1. How many different ways can 50 nickels be placed into two piles so that each pile contains at least 20 cents? (<u>43 ways</u>)

2. How many different ways can 8 pennies be placed into four sets so that each set contains at least 1 cent? (<u>35 ways</u>)

3. How many different ways can 99 dimes be placed into three boxes so that each box contains at least 10 cents?
   (<u>4753</u> = 1 + 2 + 3 + ... + 97)

3-Digit Numbers

If all the digits must be different and the sum of the digits must be odd, how many 3-digit numbers between 399 and 999 can be formed by using only the digits 0, 3, 6, and 9?

If all the digits must be different and the sum of the digits must be odd, how many 3-digit numbers between 399 and 999 can be formed by using only the digits 0, 3, 6, and 9?

Solution I Strategy: Draw a Diagram

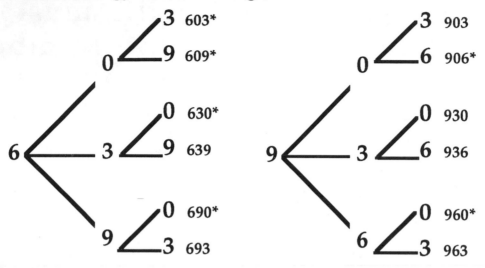

Solution II Strategy: Make an Organized List

		*	*	*	*			*	*		
Hundreds digit	6	6	6	6	6	6	9	9	9	9	9	9
Tens digit	0	3	0	9	3	9	0	3	0	6	3	6
Ones digit	3	0	9	0	9	3	3	0	6	0	6	3

There are <u>six</u> numbers (*) that satisfy all the conditions.

RELATED PROBLEMS and/or EXTENSIONS

1. If all the digits must be different, find all 3-digit even numbers less than 600 that can be written by using only the digits 1, 2, 6, and 7. (<u>126</u> <u>162</u> <u>172</u> <u>176</u> <u>216</u> <u>276</u>)

2. How many 2-digit numbers have a tens digit which is not equal to the ones digit? (<u>81</u> = 90 - 9)

3. How many 3-digit numbers are not multiples of 9? (<u>800</u> = 900 - 100)

4. How many numbers are there in the set shown below? (<u>998</u> = 1001 - 3)
   12 15 18 21 24 ... 3003

              PROBLEM SOLVING CHALLENGES

How Many Posts?

A farmer fenced in a rectangular field whose length is twice its width. He then divided the field into four equal areas by constructing a fence across the field horizontally and vertically. The area of the field is 3200 square meters, its perimeter is 240 meters, and the fence posts are all 5 meters apart. How many posts were needed to complete the job?

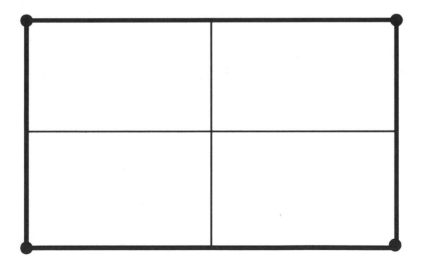

A farmer fenced in a rectangular field whose length is twice its width. He then divided the field into 4 equal areas by constructing a fence across the field horizontally and vertically. The area of the field is 3200 square meters, its perimeter is 240 meters, and the fence posts are all 5 meters apart. How many posts were needed to complete the job?

Strategies: Use a Variable   Guess and Test

Start by finding the width and length of the field.

Guess and Test	Use a Variable	Use a Variable
Area = width x length	P = Perimeter	A=width x length

width	length	area		
20	40	800	$P = 2(\text{width} + \text{length})$	$3200 = X(2X)$
30	60	1200	$240 = 2X + 4X$	$3200 = 2X^2$
40	80	3200	$240 = 6X$	$X = 40$ (width)
			$X = 40$ (width) $2X = 80$ (length)	$2X = 80$ (length)

The number of posts surrounding the field is 48. Explain why.
The number of posts inside the field is 21. Show why.
Hence, 69 posts were needed to complete the job.

RELATED PROBLEMS and/or EXTENSIONS

1. The Leung family has an 85 foot long fence along one side of their yard. It is 70 feet from the seventh post to the last post and the distance between the posts is 2.5 feet. How many posts are there? (35 posts)

2. A 50-meter by 120-meter rectangular field is bordered by a fence whose posts are all 10 meters apart. A similar fence along one of its diagonals divides the field into two equal areas. How many fence posts are there altogether? (46 posts)

Chords in a Circle

What is the largest possible number of intersecting points when nine chords are drawn inside a circle?

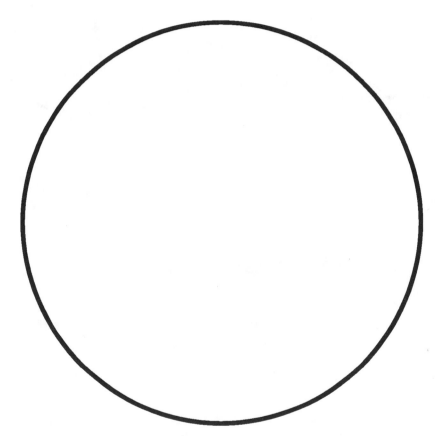

What is the largest possible number of intersecting points when nine chords are drawn inside a circle?

Strategies: Solve a Simpler Problem Make a List Look for a Pattern

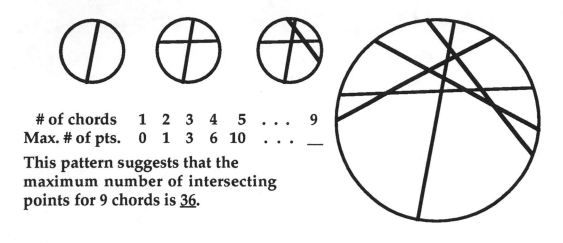

# of chords	1	2	3	4	5	. . .	9
Max. # of pts.	0	1	3	6	10	. . .	__

This pattern suggests that the maximum number of intersecting points for 9 chords is <u>36</u>.

RELATED PROBLEMS and/or EXTENSIONS

1. What is the largest possible number of intersecting points when 41 chords are drawn inside a circle? (<u>820</u> = 1 + 2 + 3 + . . . + 40)

2. What is the maximum number of regions inside a circle when nine chords are drawn inside a circle? (<u>46</u>)

3. A 4-foot wide sidewalk surrounds a rectangular flower garden of area 240 square yards and perimeter 64 yards. Find the area of the sidewalk in square feet. (<u>832 sq. ft.</u>)

4. A group of girls is standing equally spaced around a circle. The 43rd girl is directly opposite the 89th girl. How many girls are there? (<u>92</u>)

       PROBLEM SOLVING CHALLENGES

Change for a $1 bill

You are asked to make change for a $1 bill. How many different ways can this be done with ten or less coins if at least two of the coins must be quarters?

You are asked to make change for a $1 bill. How many different ways can this be done with ten or less coins if at least two of the coins must be quarters?

Strategy: Make an Organized List

Half Dollars	Quarters	Dimes	Nickels	Pennies	# of coins	Total Value
1	2	0	0	0	3	$1.00
0	2	5	0	0	7	$1.00
0	2	4	2	0	8	$1.00
0	2	3	4	0	9	$1.00
0	2	2	6	0	10	$1.00
0	3	2	1	0	6	$1.00
0	3	2	0	5	10	$1.00
0	3	1	3	0	7	$1.00
0	3	0	5	0	8	$1.00
0	4	0	0	0	4	$1.00

There are <u>10</u> different ways.

RELATED PROBLEMS and/or EXTENSIONS

1. Kim has a collection of dimes and quarters. She has seven quarters. Could the total value of her coin collection be

    $5.00? (No) $4.25? (Yes) $1.35? (No)

2. How many different ways can you make change for a $5 bill using only dimes and quarters? (<u>11 ways</u>)

3. I have five coins, each of which is a nickel, a dime, or a quarter. Also, I have at least one of each. Which of the following cannot be the total value of my coins?
    60 cents   90 cents   75 cents   55 cents   <u>80 cents</u>   70 cents

4. A box contains 9 red, 9 blue, and 9 yellow chips. Without looking, you take out one chip at a time. What is the smallest number of chips you must remove to be sure of ending up with
    a. three chips of the same color? (<u>7 chips</u>)
    b. six chips of the same color? (<u>16 chips</u>)

Patterns

A					1	2	3	4				
B				5	6	7	8	9	10			
C			11	12	13	14	15	16	17	18		
D		19	20	21	22	23	24	25	26	27	28	
E	29	30	31	32	33	34	35	36	37	38	39	40
F					·		·		·			

Suppose the pattern continues as shown above.

a. How many numbers will be in set W?

b. Which set will contain 444? 169? 670?

c. Which number will be directly above 322?

A					1	2	3	4				
B				5	6	7	8	9	10			
C			11	12	13	14	15	16	17	18		
D		19	20	21	22	23	24	25	26	27	28	
E	29	30	31	32	33	34	35	36	37	38	39	40
F					.	.	.					

Suppose the pattern continues as shown above.

A 1 B 2 C 3 D 4 E 5 F 6 G 7 H 8 I 9 J 10 K 11 L 12 M 13

O 15 P 16 Q 17 R 18 S 19 T 20 U 21 V 22 W 23 X 24 Y 25

a. How many numbers will be in set W?

W is the 23rd letter → 2(23) + 2 = __48__

b. Which set will contain 444? 169? 670?

Look at the perfect square in each set.
A (1) → 4   B (2) → 9   C (3) → 16   D (4) → 25.
Therefore, $441 = 21^2$ is in set T (20). Hence, 444 is in set T. Why?
Similarly, __169 is in set L__ and __670 is in set Y__. Why?

c. Which number will be directly above 322?

__287__   288   289 (17 x 17)

322   323   324 (18 x 18)

RELATED PROBLEMS and/or EXTENSIONS

In the pattern shown above:

a. what is the first number in set T? (__419__ = 20 x 20 + 20 - 1)

b. what is the 14th number in set K? (__144__ = 12 x 12)

c. what is the sum of the numbers in set T?
(419+420+421+...+460 = 21 x 879 = __18,459__)

PROBLEM SOLVING CHALLENGES

Bookworm

Each book in a five-volume set is 4 cm thick. This includes the covers which are each 0.3 cm thick. If a bookworm starts on the first page of volume 1 and eats its way through the last page of volume 5, how far will the worm have traveled?

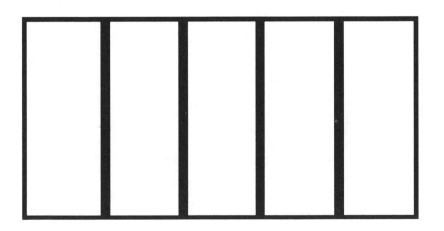

Each book in a five-volume set is 4 cm thick. This includes the covers which are each 0.3 cm thick. If a bookworm starts on the first page of volume 1 and eats its way through to the last page of volume 5, how far will the worm have traveled?

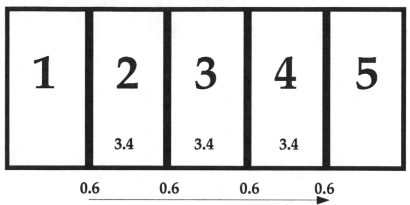

Strategy: Use a Model (books)

Distance = (4 x 0.6 + 3 x 3.4) cm = <u>12.6 cm</u>

RELATED PROBLEMS and/or EXTENSIONS

1. Assuming the same conditions as stated in the above problem, how far will the worm have traveled in a 26-volume set of books?
An N-volume set of books?
<u>96.6 cm</u> = 25x0.6 + 24x3.4   <u>0.6(N-1) + 3.4(N-2)</u>

2. If 24 cubes (each of which has a volume of 8 cubic centimeters) are arranged to form a rectangular solid, what is its smallest possible surface area in square centimeters? (<u>54 sq. cm</u> → 2x3x4)
What is its largest possible surface area? (<u>144 sq. cm</u> → 1x1x24)

3. The elevators in a 39-floor building travel at a constant speed. If it takes 20 seconds for each elevator to travel from the first floor to the ninth floor, how long will it take one of the elevators to go from the middle floor to the top floor? (<u>47.5 seconds</u>)

            PROBLEM SOLVING CHALLENGES

Chips Game

Juanita and Carla each has a set of chips. They decided to play four rounds of a game where, after each round, the loser must give the winner as many chips as the winner has at that time. Both girls ended up with 16 chips. If Juanita won the first two rounds and Carla won the last two rounds, how many chips did each one have at the start?

Juanita and Carla each has a set of chips. They decided to play four rounds of a game where, after each round, the loser must give the winner as many chips as the winner has at that time. Both girls ended up with 16 chips. If Juanita won the first two rounds and Carla won the last two rounds, how many chips did each one have at the start?

Solution I Strategy: Work Backward

	After game 4	After game 3	After game 2	After game 1	Start
Juanita	16	24	28	14	7
Carla	16	8	4	18	25

Carla had 25 chips and Juanita had 7 chips.

Solution II Strategy: Use a Variable

		Carla	Juanita
Start →		X	Y
After Round 1		X-Y	2Y
After Round 2		X-3Y	4Y
After Round 3		2X-6Y	4Y-(X-3Y) = 7Y - X
After Round 4		4X-12Y	7Y-X-(2X-6Y) = 13Y - 3X
		4X-12Y = 16	13Y-3X = 16

Solve these equations to show that X = 25 and Y = 7.
Carla had 25 chips and Juanita had 7 chips.

RELATED PROBLEMS and/or EXTENSIONS

1. Bonita and Greg are playing a game where they take turns removing either one or two chips from a pile of chips. The person who removes the last chips wins the game. Suppose it is Bonita's turn and there are 14 chips left. Find a strategy that will make her a sure winner.
   (Chips left after Bonita's turn: 12, 9, 6, 3)

2. Lonnie spent all but $3.00 of her savings in three stores. In each store, she spent $4.00 more than half of what she had when she went in. How much money did Lonnie have at the start? ($80.00)

           PROBLEM SOLVING CHALLENGES

Volleyball

Four Volleyball teams A, B, C, and D in the Midwest Conference played each other one home game and one away game last season. Find the won-lost record for each team given the below clues.

- B won all of its home games
- A never defeated C
- C lost two games, both of which were away games
- A had its only win at home
- B lost only one game

Four Volleyball teams A, B, C, and D in the Midwest Conference played each other one home game and one away game last season. Find the won-lost record for each team given the below clues.

- B won all of its home games
- A never defeated C
- C lost two games, both of which were away games
- A had its only win at home
- B lost only one game

Strategy: Make an Organized List

Find the winners using the given clues

Home A	<u>B</u>	A	<u>C</u>	<u>A</u>	D	<u>B</u>	C	B	D	<u>C</u>	<u>D</u>
Away	<u>B</u>	A	<u>C</u>	A	D	A	C	B	D	<u>B</u>	D	C

	A	B	C	D
Won	1	5	4	2
Lost	5	1	2	4

RELATED PROBLEMS and/or EXTENSIONS

1. Three softball teams (A, B, C) played each other in home and away games. Find the won-lost record for each team using the below clues:
   A lost 2 games to B   C lost 2 games   C won all its home games
   (Won/Lost: A 1/3 B 3/1 C 2/2)

2. Find two different 8-digit numbers made up with the digits 1, 1, 2, 2, 3, 3, 4, and 4 such that all of the below conditions hold true.
   The 1's are separated by one digit
   The 2's are separated by two digits
   The 3's are separated by three digits, and
   The 4's are separated by four digits   (<u>23421314</u>   <u>41312432</u>)

3. I am a 2-digit odd counting number divisible by 3. If I am multiplied by 4 and then increased by 3, the answer is greater than 70 and less than 110. Who am I? (<u>21</u>)

      PROBLEM SOLVING CHALLENGES

Don't Spill a Drop!

Suppose you have an 8-liter container that is filled with water. You also have an empty 3-liter container and an empty 5-liter container. Without spilling a drop, show how these containers can be used to measure out exactly 4 liters of water.

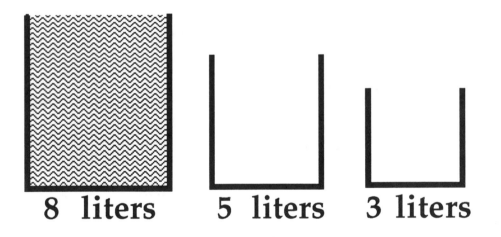

8 liters   5 liters   3 liters

Suppose you have an 8-liter container that is filled with water. You also have an empty 3-liter container and an empty 5-liter container. Without spilling a drop, show how these containers can be used to measure out exactly 4 liters of water.

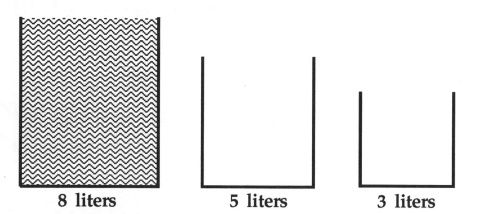

| | | 8 liters | | 5 liters | | 3 liters |

Strategies: Guess and Test Make a List

	Start	1st	2nd	3rd	4th	5th	6th	7th
8-liter container	8	5	5	2	2	7	7	4
5-liter container	0	0	3	3	5	0	1	1
3-liter container	0	3	0	3	1	1	0	3

RELATED PROBLEMS and/or EXTENSIONS

1. Show how you can end up with exactly 6 liters of water when starting with empty 3-liter and 5-liter containers and an 8-liter container that is full of water. (0 0 8 → 0 5 3 → 3 2 3 → 0 2 <u>6</u>)

2. Sharon has two 20-ounce cups full of water. She also has an empty 8-ounce cup and an empty 14-ounce cup. Using only these four cups, she wants to end up with exactly 6 ounces of water in each of the smaller cups. Without spilling a drop, how can this be done?
(20 20 0 0→20 12 8 0→20 0 8 12→18 0 8 14→18 8 0 14→18 8 8 6→20 8 <u>6</u> <u>6</u>)

    PROBLEM SOLVING CHALLENGES

Diagonals

Every quadrilateral (4-gon) has 2 diagonals, every hexagon (6-gon) has 9 diagonals, and every octagon (8-gon) has 20 diagonals. Verify!

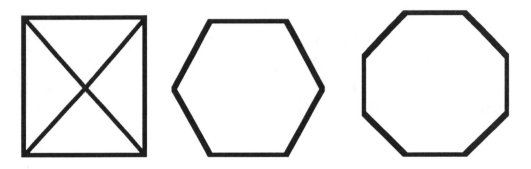

How many diagonals does each of the following polygons have?

a. Decagon (10-gon)
b. Dodecagon (12-gon)

Every quadrilateral (4-gon) has 2 diagonals, every hexagon (6-gon) has 9 diagonals, and every octagon (8-gon) has 20 diagonals. Verify!

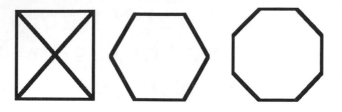

How many diagonals does each of the following polygons have?
a. Decagon (10-gon)
b. Dodecagon (12-gon)

Strategies: Solve a Simpler Problem Make a List Look for a Pattern

# of sides	3	4	5	6	7	8	...
# of diagonals	0	2	5	9	14	20	...
Differences		2	3	4	5	6	

The above pattern suggests: 10-gon → 35 diagonals   12-gon → 54 diagonals

---

RELATED PROBLEMS and/or EXTENSIONS

1. How many diagonals does a 15-gon have? (90)

2. In how many different ways can 100 quarters be placed into two disjoint sets given that each set of coins must contain at least $1.00? (93 ways)
How many different ways for N quarters if N ≥ 8? (N - 7 ways)

3. What is the degree measure of each angle of a regular
a. Decagon? (144)   b. 20-gon? (162)   c. N-gon? $180(N - 2)/N$

4. What is the MAXIMUM number of regions into which each of the following can divide a circle?
a. 50 radii (50)   b. 50 diameters (100)   c. 10 chords (56)
d. N radii (N)   e. N diameters (2N)   f. N chords ($N^2/2 + N/2 + 1$)

Coins in a Square

How can 4 pennies, 4 nickels, 4 dimes, and 4 quarters be arranged in a 4x4 array so that the value of the coins in each row, column, and diagonal is the same?

How can 4 pennies, 4 nickels, 4 dimes, and 4 quarters be arranged in a 4x4 array so that the value of the coins in each row, column, and diagonal is the same?

<u>Strategies:</u> Guess and Test   Use a Model

One of several possible solutions is shown below.

P	N	D	Q
D	Q	P	N
Q	D	N	P
N	P	Q	D

RELATED PROBLEMS and/or EXTENSIONS

1. Show how 3 pennies, 3 dimes, and 3 quarters can be arranged in a 3 by 3 square array so that the value of the coins in each row and column is different.

   Row 1: Q P Q   Row 2: D D D   Row 3: P P Q

2. How can 4 pennies, 4 nickels, 4 dimes, and 4 quarters be arranged in a 4 by 4 square array so that the value of the coins in each row, column, and diagonal is different?

   Row 1: P N P N   Row 2: D N D Q
   Row 3: Q P P N   Row 4: D Q Q D

   There are other possible solutions.

            PROBLEM SOLVING CHALLENGES

Cows and Turkeys

In a group of cows and turkeys, the number of heads is 52 less than the number of legs. What is the largest number of cows that could be in this group of animals?

In a group of cows and turkeys, the number of heads is 52 less than the number of legs. What is the largest number of cows that could be in this group of animals?

Strategy: Use a Variable

Let C = # of cows and let T = # of turkeys

\# of legs = 4C + 2T   \# of heads = C + T

(4C + 2T) - (C + T) = 52 $\Rightarrow$ 3C + T = 52

Hence, the maximum possible number of cows is <u>17</u>. Why?

RELATED PROBLEMS and/or EXTENSIONS

1. After being warned about the dangers of smoking, a man decided to cut back smoking at the rate of 3 cigarettes a day for one week. If he smoked 196 cigarettes during that week, how many did he smoke the day before he started to cut back? (<u>40</u>)

2. Glenda has a 2:30 p.m. appointment with a client in Richfield. Before leaving home, she figured that if she drives at an average of 60 mph, she will get there 30 minutes early, and if she drives at an average of 30 mph, she will arrive 20 minutes late. How many miles is it from Glenda's house to Richfield?
(<u>50 miles</u>: D/30 - D/60 = 5/6 $\Rightarrow$ D = 50)

3. What is Big Al's weight given that he weighs 124 pounds plus half his weight?
(<u>248 pounds</u>: N = N/2 + 124 $\Rightarrow$ N = 248)

4. Suppose a train traveling at a constant rate of 60 mph takes nine seconds for it to enter a tunnel. From there it takes 63 seconds before the train is completely outside the tunnel. Find the length of both the train and the tunnel.
(Train length = <u>0.15 mile</u>   Tunnel length = 6 x 0.15 = <u>0.9 mile</u>)

Even Whole Numbers

Jennifer wrote a list of consecutive even whole numbers starting with the number 2. She wrote 211 digits. What was the last 3-digit number she wrote?

2   4   6   8   10   12   14   16 . . .

Jennifer wrote a list of consecutive even whole numbers starting with the number 2. She wrote 211 digits. What was the last 3-digit number she wrote?

Strategy: Make a List

2, 4, 6, 8,	4 digits
10, 12, 14, . . . , 98	90 digits (90 = 2 x 45). Why?
100, 102, 104, . . .	211 - 94 = 117 more digits are needed.

Therefore, 39 3-digit even numbers are needed. Why?
Hence, the last 3-digit number was <u>176</u>. Why?

RELATED PROBLEMS and/or EXTENSIONS

1. How many digits will be needed to number the pages of a book that contains
   a. 101 pages?   (<u>195 digits</u>)
   b. 999 pages?   (<u>2889 digits</u>)

2. How many digits are there in each of the below number sequences?
   a. 8, 9, 10, 11, . . . , 189   (<u>452</u> = 2 + 180 + 270)
   b. 25, 50, 75, 100, 125, . . . , 1000   (<u>118</u> = 6 + 3x36 + 4)

3. What is the 88th term in each of the following sequences?
   a. 8, 9, 10, 11, . . .   (<u>95</u> = 88 + 7)
   b. 4, 6, 8, 10, . . .   (<u>178</u> = 2x88 + 2)

         PROBLEM SOLVING CHALLENGES

Cube Patterns

All of the below 6-square patterns can be folded to form a cubical box. Which face (X) will be opposite ■ and which face (Y) will be opposite ▨?

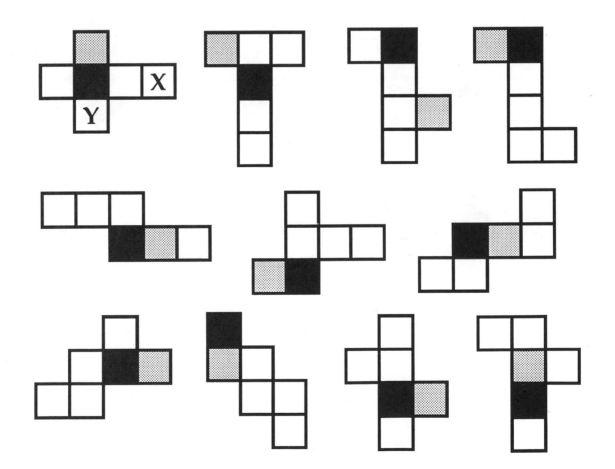

All of the below 6-square patterns can be folded to form a cubical box. Which face (X) will be opposite ■, and which face (Y) will be opposite ▨?

Strategy: Use a Model

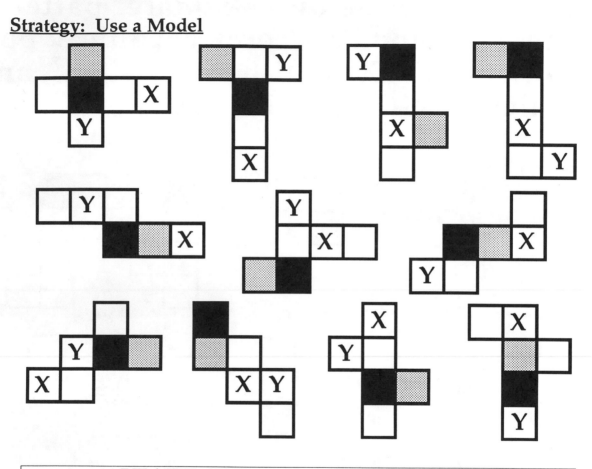

RELATED PROBLEMS and/or EXTENSIONS

1. Draw the <u>twelve</u> 5-square patterns. ...

2. How many of these patterns will fold into an open top box? (<u>8</u>)
   For each pattern that would fold into a box, write B in the square that would be the bottom of the box.

3. How many of the 5-square patterns have at least one line of symmetry? (<u>6</u>)

4. How many of the 5-square patterns have either 90-degree or 180-degree rotational symmetry? (<u>3</u>)

Bank Account

The Federal Savings Bank offers the following checking account plans:

Plan A: $4.00 monthly fee plus 15 cents per check

Plan B: $2.00 monthly fee plus 20 cents per check

Plan C: 30 cents per check with no monthly fee

Under what conditions should a customer select plan A? plan B? plan C?

The Federal Savings Bank offers the following checking account plans:

Plan A: $4.00 monthly fee plus 15 cents per check

Plan B: $2.00 monthly fee plus 20 cents per check

Plan C: 30 cents per check with no monthly fee

Under what conditions should a customer select plan A?   plan B?   plan C?

Strategy: Make an Organized List

# of checks	Plan A	Plan B	Plan C
0	$4.00	$2.00	$0.00
10	$5.50	$4.00	$3.00
20	$7.00	$6.00	$6.00
30	$8.50	$8.00	$9.00
40	$10.00	$10.00	$12.00
50	$11.50	$12.00	$15.00

Plan A is the best choice when a customer writes more than 40 checks per month.

Plan B is the best choice when a customer writes between 19 and 41 checks per month.

Plan C is the best choice when a customer writes less than 20 checks per month.

RELATED PROBLEMS and/or EXTENSIONS

1. What will be the bank charges for 26 checks for a customer that selects:

   plan A? ($7.90)   plan B? ($7.20)   plan C? ($7.80)

2. A certain bank now charges a monthly fee of $2 for checking accounts plus 12 cents for each check. The bank advertises a new plan where the monthly fee is $3 and the cost per check is 9 cents. What is the least number of checks a customer must write before the new plan is cheaper than the plan they now offer? (34 checks)

 © 1993 TRICON Publishing   PROBLEM SOLVING CHALLENGES

Line Segments

The figure shown below has eight points on a line between P and Q. How many different line segments are there?

The figure shown below has eight points on a line between P and Q. How many different line segments are there?

P ●————●——●——●————●——●——●————● Q

Solution I Strategies: Solve a Simpler Problem Make a List
Look for a Pattern

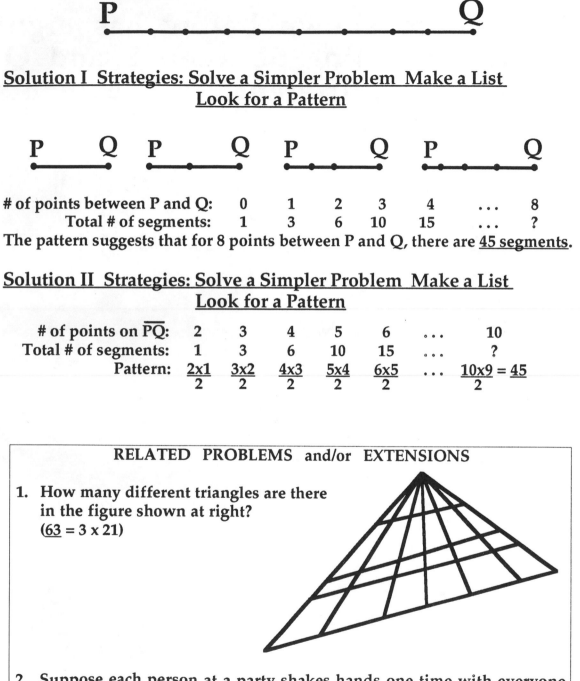

P ●●● Q   P ●—●—● Q   P ●—●●—● Q   P ●—●●●—● Q

# of points between P and Q:	0	1	2	3	4	...	8
Total # of segments:	1	3	6	10	15	...	?

The pattern suggests that for 8 points between P and Q, there are <u>45 segments</u>.

Solution II Strategies: Solve a Simpler Problem Make a List
Look for a Pattern

# of points on $\overline{PQ}$:	2	3	4	5	6	...	10
Total # of segments:	1	3	6	10	15	...	?
Pattern:	$\frac{2 \times 1}{2}$	$\frac{3 \times 2}{2}$	$\frac{4 \times 3}{2}$	$\frac{5 \times 4}{2}$	$\frac{6 \times 5}{2}$	...	$\frac{10 \times 9}{2} = \underline{45}$

RELATED PROBLEMS and/or EXTENSIONS

1. How many different triangles are there in the figure shown at right?
   (<u>63</u> = 3 x 21)

2. Suppose each person at a party shakes hands one time with everyone else. There were 55 handshakes. How many people were there? (<u>11</u>)

Black and White Chips

There are 24 chips in the set below.

How many white chips should be removed from the set of chips so that:

a. 1/4 of the remaining chips are white?

b. 2/3 of the remaining chips are not white?

c. 40% of the remaining chips are white?

d. 80% of the remaining chips are not white?

There are 24 chips in the set below.

How many white chips should be removed from the set of chips so that:
a. 1/4 of the remaining chips are white?
b. 2/3 of the remaining chips are not white?
c. 40% of the remaining chips are white?
d. 80% of the remaining chips are not white?

Strategy: Use a Variable

Let X be the # of white chips removed.

a. (12 - X)/(24 - X) = 1/4 ⇒ X = 8

b. (12 - X)/(24 - X) = 1/3 ⇒ X = 6

c. (12 - X)/(24 - X) = 2/5 ⇒ X = 4

d. (12 - X)/(24 - X) = 1/5 ⇒ X = 9

Alternate Strategy: Use a Model (Chips)

RELATED PROBLEMS and/or EXTENSIONS
1. The teacher-to-student ratio in a school system which has 9,240 students is 1 to 28. How many new teachers should the district hire to reduce the ratio to 1 to 22? (90 teachers)
2. Suppose four men can plant eight trees in six hours. Working at this rate, how many hours will it take three men to plant nine trees? (9 hours)
3. Suppose 3 chickens lay 6 eggs in a day and a half. At this rate, how many eggs will 12 chickens lay in 12 days? (192 eggs)

Grazing Area

A goat is tied to the corner of a 40-foot by 30-foot barn with a 50-foot rope. If the goat can graze everywhere outside the barn that the rope allows it to reach, what is the grazing area?

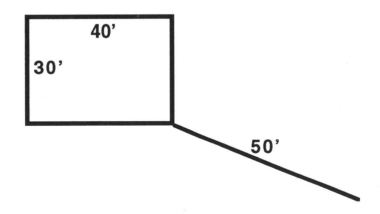

A goat is tied to the corner of a 40-foot by 30-foot barn with a 50-foot rope. If the goat can graze everywhere outside the barn that the rope allows it to reach, what is the grazing area?

Strategy: Draw a Diagram

Recall: Area of a circle = πr^2
Area of region A is 100π
Area of region B is 625π
Area of region C is 1250π
Area of region D is 25π

Total grazing area is <u>2,000π sq. feet</u>

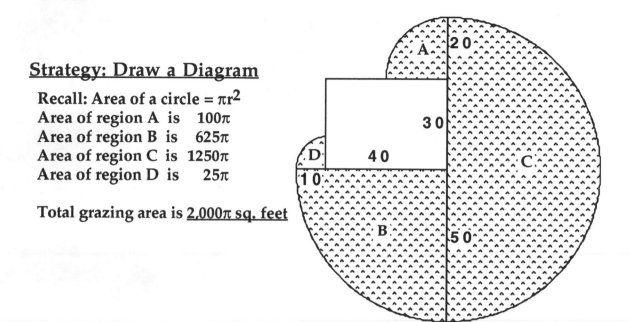

RELATED PROBLEMS and/or EXTENSIONS

1. A horse, inside a fenced-in square field, is tied to a corner post with a 20-meter long rope. If the field has an area of 900 square meters, which of the following best represents the grazing area that the horse cannot reach?

   220 m^2 340 m^2 460 m^2 <u>580 m^2</u>

2. Which of the following best represents the area of a regular hexagon whose perimeter is 24 cm?

   23 cm^2 <u>43 cm^2</u>   73 cm^2 93 cm^2

$666,666,666^2$

$666,666,666^2$ is equal to an 18-digit number. What is the sum of its digits?

666,666,666^2 is equal to an 18-digit number. What is the sum of its digits?

Strategies: Solve a Simpler Problem Make a List Look for a Pattern

Term:	$6^2 = 36$	$66^2 = 4356$	$666^2 = 443556$	$6666^2 = 44435556$	. . .
Sum of digits:	$9 = 9 \times 1$	$18 = 9 \times 2$	$27 = 9 \times 3$	$36 = 9 \times 4$	. . .

The above pattern suggests that 666,666,666^2 has <u>81</u> as the sum of its digits.

Extension: What is the sum of the digits in the answer for
555 x 999,999,999? (<u>81</u>)

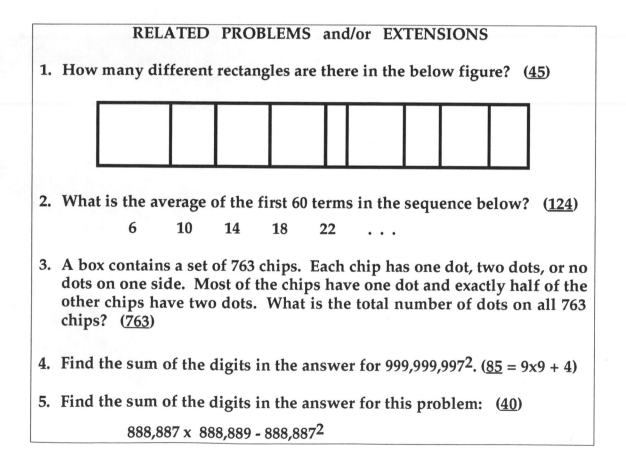

RELATED PROBLEMS and/or EXTENSIONS

1. How many different rectangles are there in the below figure? (<u>45</u>)

2. What is the average of the first 60 terms in the sequence below? (<u>124</u>)

      6   10   14   18   22   . . .

3. A box contains a set of 763 chips. Each chip has one dot, two dots, or no dots on one side. Most of the chips have one dot and exactly half of the other chips have two dots. What is the total number of dots on all 763 chips? (<u>763</u>)

4. Find the sum of the digits in the answer for 999,999,997^2. (<u>85</u> = 9 x 9 + 4)

5. Find the sum of the digits in the answer for this problem: (<u>40</u>)

     888,887 x 888,889 - 888,887^2

     PROBLEM SOLVING CHALLENGES

Balance Scale

Suppose you have nineteen chips and a balance scale. The chips are identical, except that one is slightly heavier than the other chips. Show how to find the heavier chip in three or less weighings on the balance scale.

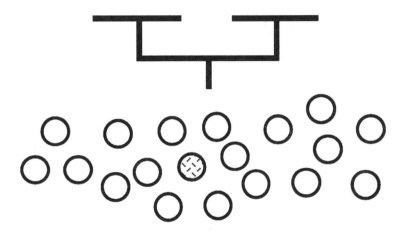

Suppose you have nineteen chips and a balance scale. The chips are identical, except that one is slightly heavier than the other chips. Show how to find the heavier chip in three or less weighings on the balance scale.

Strategies: <u>Use a Model   Draw a Diagram</u>

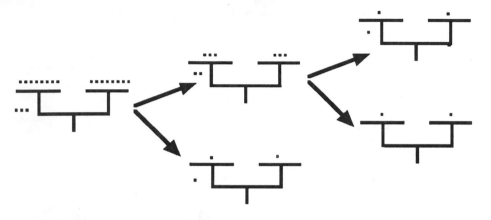

The above diagram shows how you can be sure of finding the chip with three or less weighings on a balance scale. Explain why.

RELATED PROBLEMS and/or EXTENSIONS

1. Under the conditions stated in the problem above, what is the least number of weighings that will be needed on a balance scale to be sure of finding one slightly heavier chip given that there is a total of 27 chips? (<u>3 weighings</u>)   A total of 82 chips? (<u>5 weighings</u>)

2. Suppose you have some coins and a balance scale. The coins are identical except that one of them is counterfeit and either slightly heavier or slightly lighter than the other coins. How many weighings will be needed to be sure of finding the counterfeit coin and determining whether it is lighter or heavier than the other coins given that you start with
    a. 5 coins? (<u>3</u>)   b. 12 coins? (<u>5</u>)

Clues

Use the below clues to find the number represented by each letter.

* Each letter represents a different 1-digit whole number

* The 4 corner numbers are all odd

* The sum of the 2 middle numbers is 9

* The sum of A and D is 6

* D x E x F = 0

* A + B + C = 13

A B C
D E F

Use the below clues to find the number represented by each letter.
* Each letter represents a different 1-digit whole number
* The 4 corner numbers are all odd
* The sum of the 2 middle numbers is 9
* The sum of A and D is 6
* D x E x F = 0
* A + B + C = 13

Strategies: Guess and Test Make a List

A_1 B_9 C_3

D_5 E_0 F_7

RELATED PROBLEMS and/or EXTENSIONS

1. Use the clues below to find the number represented by each letter.
   * All are different 1-digit whole numbers.
   * The corner numbers are all even.
   * F is less than C and C x F = 0.
   * ABC is a 3-digit number divisible by 9.
   * D is a prime number.
   * A + D = 10 and B + E = 13.
   * E is one more than the average of A, B, and C.

   A   B   C

   D   E   F

   (A = 8   B = 6   C = 4   D = 2   E = 7   F = 0)

2. Use the clues below to find the number represented by each letter.
   * All are different 1-digit whole numbers.
   * The sum of all the numbers is 29.
   * Three of the corner numbers are odd.
   * The product of A and D is 10.
   * D is an even number.

   A   B   C

   D   E   F

   (A = 5   B = 8   C = 9   D = 2   E = 4   F = 1)

PROBLEM SOLVING CHALLENGES

Crossing a River

Five men and three boys want to cross a river using a small raft that holds either one man or two boys. What is the least number of times that the raft must cross the river to get everybody to the other side?

M M M M M
B B B

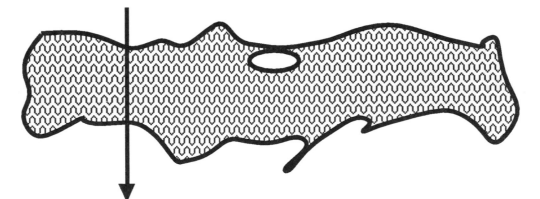

Five men and three boys want to cross a river using a small raft that holds either one man or two boys. What is the least number of times that the raft must cross the river to get everybody to the other side?

Strategies: Draw a Diagram   Use a Model

Find the number of crossings needed to get one man across the river and return the raft to the starting point.

Two boys cross. One boy brings the raft back. One man crosses. The other boy brings the raft back to the starting point. Now the raft is where it started and one man is across the river. <u>4 crossings needed</u>.

Hence, it will take 20 (4 x 5) trips to get the 5 men across the river and have the raft back at the starting point. Two more crossings will now be needed to get the 3 boys to the other side. Therefore, it will take 22 crossings to get everyone to the other side.

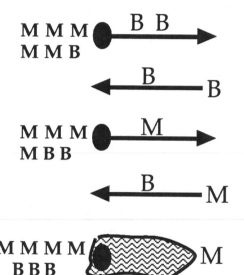

RELATED PROBLEMS and/or EXTENSIONS

1. How many crossings of the river would be needed if there were 7 men and 2 boys? (<u>29</u>)

2. Under the conditions stated in the problem, would it be possible for six men and one boy to cross the river? Explain why or why not. (<u>No</u>)

Diagonal Length

Suppose that the rectangular field ABCD represented below has an area of 768 square meters and a perimeter of 112 meters. What is the length of diagonal AC?

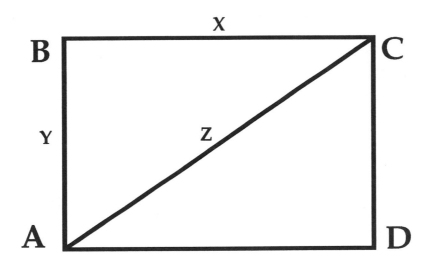

Suppose that the rectangular field ABCD represented below has an area of 768 square meters and a perimeter of 112 meters. What is the length of diagonal AC?

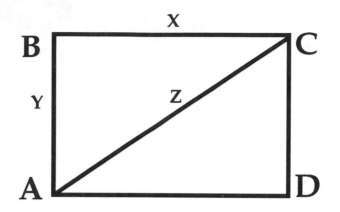

<u>Strategies: Guess and Test   Make a List</u>

First determine X and Y. Note that $X + Y = 56$. Why?

Guess → X	Y	XY		
28	28	784	no	$Z^2 = X^2 + Y^2$
20	36	720	no	$= 24^2 + 32^2 = 1600$
. . .				$\therefore AC = \underline{40 \text{ meters}}$
24	32	768	yes	

RELATED PROBLEMS and/or EXTENSIONS

1. A rectangular field has a perimeter of 200 meters and an area of 2,356 square meters. What are its dimensions?
   (<u>38 m by 62 m</u>)

2. A rectangular flower garden of area 836 square feet is surrounded by a fence of length 120 feet. What are the dimensions of the garden?
   (<u>38 feet by 22 feet</u>)

3. Suppose six equally spaced points on a circle are joined to form a regular hexagon of perimeter 12 centimeters. Which of the following best represents the difference, in square centimeters, between the area of the circle and the area of the hexagon?   1.8   2.0   <u>2.2</u>   2.4   2.6

PROBLEM SOLVING CHALLENGES

Look for a Pattern

Find the next three terms in each set below:

a.   1, 1, 2, 3, 5, 8   b.   1, 3, 6, 10, 15

c.   1, 8, 27, 64   d.   0, 3, 8, 15, 24

Find the Nth term in the sequence
     0, 3, 8, 15, 24, ...

Make a List

Elita has a collection of dimes and quarters worth \$4.00. Which of the following cannot be the total number of coins in her collection?

19   25   28   31   33

Look for a Pattern
Find the next three terms in each set below:

a. 1,1,2,3,5,8, <u>13</u> , <u>21</u> , <u>34</u>
Each term after the second is
the sum of the previous two terms.

b. 1,3,6,10,15, <u>21</u> , <u>28</u> , <u>36</u>
The differences are 2, 3, 4, 5, 6, . . .

c. 1,8,27,64, <u>125</u> , <u>216</u> , <u>343</u>
The terms are the cubes of the
counting numbers.

d. 0,3,8,15,24, <u>35</u> , <u>48</u> , <u>63</u>
The differences are 3, 5, 7, 9, 11, . . .

Find the Nth term in the sequence
0, 3, 8, 15, 24, ... <u>$(N^2 - 1)$</u>

Make a List
Elita has a collection of dimes and quarters worth $4.00. Which of the following cannot be the total number of coins in her collection?

19   25   28   31   33

# of Dimes	40	35	30	25	20	15	10	5	0
# of Quarters	0	2	4	6	8	10	12	14	16
# of coins	40	37	34	31	28	25	22	19	16

Elita cannot have <u>33</u> coins.

   PROBLEM SOLVING CHALLENGES

Solve a Simpler Problem

How many different rectangles are in the below figure?

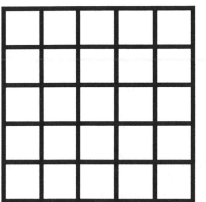

Draw a Diagram

Starting at one corner, the boundary of a garden runs 40 feet east, 16 feet north, 52 feet west, and then straight back to the first corner. Find the area and the perimeter of the garden.

Solve a Simpler Problem

How many different rectangles are in the below figure?

Dimension	# of rectangles
□ 1x1	1
2x2	9
3x3	36
4x4	100

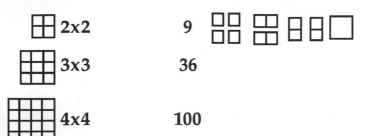

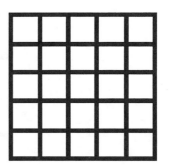

The pattern suggests that there are **225 rectangles**.

Alternate Strategy: Make a List

Size	1x1	2x1	3x1	4x1	5x1	2x2	3x2	4x2	5x2	3x3	4x3	5x3	4x4	5x4	5x5
# of rect.	25	40	30	20	10	16	24	16	8	9	12	6	4	4	1

Total number of rectangles = **225**

Extension: Solve the problem above for a 6x6 figure (**441**)
and for a 9x9 figure (**2025**).

Draw a Diagram

Starting at one corner, the boundary of a garden runs 40 feet east, 16 feet north, 52 feet west, and then straight back to the first corner. Find the area and the perimeter of the garden.

$AB^2 = 12^2 + 16^2$. Why?

$\therefore AB = 20$

Perimeter = 40+16+52+20 = **128 feet**

Area = area of rectangle + area of triangle
= 40 x 16 + 1/2(12 x 16)
= **736 square feet**

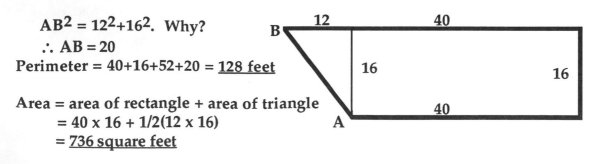

      PROBLEM SOLVING CHALLENGES

Guess and Test

The length and width of a certain rectangular field are both whole numbers. Find its dimensions given that it has an area of 966 square meters and a perimeter of 134 meters.

Use a Variable

At halftime of a basketball game, the Huskies and the Eagles were tied. During the second half the Huskies scored 61 points and the Eagles scored one more than they scored during the first half. If the Huskies won by 6 points, what was the final score?

Guess and Test

The length and width of a certain rectangular field are both whole numbers. Find its dimensions given that it has an area of 966 square meters and a perimeter of 134 meters.

Since the perimeter is 134 meters, Length + Width = 67. Why?

Length (L)	Width (W)	Area (L x W)	
50	17	850	too small
40	27	1080	too large
45	22	990	no
44	23	1012	no
46	21	966	yes

<u>Length = 46 meters</u>   <u>Width = 21 meters</u>

Use a Variable

At halftime of a basketball game, the Huskies and the Eagles were tied. During the second half the Huskies scored 61 points and the Eagles scored one more than they scored during the first half. If the Huskies won by 6 points, what was the final score?

Let N = Eagles score at halftime

	Huskies	Eagles
1st half score	N	N
2nd half score	61	N+1

Since the Huskies won by 6 points, 61 - (N+1) = 6.

Therefore, N = 54.

Final score: <u>Huskies 115</u> <u>Eagles 109</u>

               PROBLEM SOLVING CHALLENGES

Work Backward

Vince has a collection of baseball cards. He gave one more than half of the cards to his brother. He then gave his sister one less than half of the remaining cards, after which he ended up with only ten cards. How many baseball cards did Vince have in his original collection?

Use a Model

Suppose an open top cubical box is filled with 512 equal sized cubes. How many of the cubes do not touch either a side or the bottom of the box?

Work Backward

Vince has a collection of baseball cards. He gave one more than half of the cards to his brother. He then gave his sister one less than half of the remaining cards, after which he ended up with only ten cards. How many baseball cards did Vince have in his original collection?

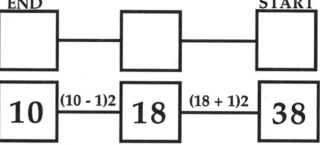

END   START

| 10 | (10 - 1)2 | 18 | (18 + 1)2 | 38 |

Vince had <u>38 cards</u> in his collection.

Use a Model

Suppose an open top cubical box is filled with 512 equal sized cubes. How many of the cubes do not touch either a side or the bottom of the box?

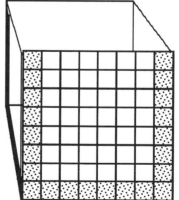

Dimensions of box = 8 x 8 x 8. Why?
Remove each row of cubes touching a side or the bottom of the box.
This leaves 6 x 6 x 7 cubes. Why?
Thus <u>252</u> cubes do not touch a side or the bottom.

<u>Alternate Solution</u>:
Remove the side facing you: 8 x 8 = 64.
Remove the side away from you: 8 x 8 = 64.
Remove the left side: 8 x 6 = 48 (why 8 x 6?)
Remove the right side: 8 x 6 = 48.
Remove the bottom: 6 x 6 = 36 (why 6 x 6?)
Thus <u>252</u> (512 - 260) cubes do not touch a side or the bottom of the box.

Five teams (A B C D E) in the All-Star softball league played each other at home and away. Use the below clues to help you find the won/lost record for each team.

  *A won all of its home games

  *B never defeated A or E

  *C lost all of its home games

  *D ended the season with 5 wins, 3 at home

  *E had 6 more wins than losses

  *C lost 2 more games than B

I am thinking of a one-digit whole number whose square is 96 less than 20 times my number. What is my number?

Five teams (A   B   C   D   E) in the All-Star softball league played each other at home and away. Use the below clues to help you find the won/lost record for each team.

    *A won all of its home games

    *B never defeated A or E

    *C lost all of its home games

    *D ended the season with 5 wins, 3 at home

    *E had 6 more wins than losses

    *C lost 2 more games than B

Strategy: Make a List

Home <u>A</u> B <u>A</u> C <u>A</u> D <u>A</u> E B C B <u>D</u> B E C <u>D</u> C E D <u>E</u>
Away B <u>A</u> C <u>A</u> D A E A C <u>B</u> D B E B D C E C <u>E</u> D

	A	B	C	D	E
Won	6	2	0	5	7
Lost	2	6	8	3	1

I am thinking of a one-digit whole number whose square is 96 less than 20 times my number. What is my number?

Strategies: Use a Variable   Guess and Test

Let X be the number.

X	20X	X^2	$20X-X^2 = 96$?	
4	80	16	64	no
6	120	36	104	no
. . .				
8	160	64	96	YES

The number is <u>8</u>.

Extension: Find the two-digit whole number that satisfies the
               conditions of the problem. (<u>12</u>)

    PROBLEM SOLVING CHALLENGES

Al, Ben, and Carl want to cross a river in a raft that will sink with a total weight that is more than 300 pounds. Their weights are 140, 155, and 195 pounds, respectively. What is the least number of crossings needed to get all of them to the other side? Explain your method.

What is the sum of the digits in the answer for 55,555 x 999,999?

Al, Ben, and Carl want to cross a river in a raft that will sink with a total weight that is more than 300 pounds. Their weights are 140, 155, and 195 pounds, respectively. What is the least number of crossings needed to get all of them to the other side? Explain your method.

Strategies: Draw a Diagram   Use a Model

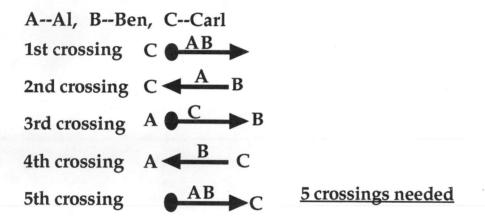

A--Al, B--Ben, C--Carl

1st crossing   C ●——AB——▶

2nd crossing   C ◀——A—— B

3rd crossing   A ●——C——▶ B

4th crossing   A ◀——B—— C

5th crossing   ●——AB——▶ C   5 crossings needed

What is the sum of the digits in the answer for 55,555 x 999,999?

Strategies: Solve a Simpler Problem Make a List Look for a Pattern

5 x 99 = 495	55 x 999 = 54945	555 x 9999 = 5549445
Sum = 18	Sum = 27	Sum = 36

The pattern suggests that the sum of the digits in 55,555 x 999,999 is 54. Why?

From a pile of 11 chips, two players take turns removing 1 chip or 4 chips. The player that removes the last chip is the winner. Find a way that will make the first player a sure winner. Explain your strategy.

How many triangles of perimeter 13 inches are there, given that the length of the sides are counting numbers?

From a pile of 11 chips, two players take turns removing 1 chip or 4 chips. The player that removes the last chip is the winner. Find a way that will make the first player a sure winner. Explain your strategy.

Strategy: Work Backward

Start: | 1st Player (takes 1) | 10 chips left | | |
| --- | --- | --- | --- |
| 2nd Player (takes 1) | 9 chips left | or (takes 4) | 6 left |
| 1st Player (takes 4) | 5 chips left | or (takes 1) | 5 left |

The first player can now be a sure winner. Explain why.

Extension: Which player can be a sure winner if the pile contains 16 chips? (<u>Second player</u>)

How many triangles of perimeter 13 inches are there, given that the length of the sides are counting numbers?

Strategy: Make a List

Let X, Y, and Z be the lengths of the sides of each possible triangle.

					*		*		*	*	*	
X	1	1	1	1	1	1	2	2	2	2	3	3	3	4
Y	1	2	3	4	5	6	2	3	4	5	3	4	5	4
Z	11	10	9	8	7	6	9	8	7	6	7	6	5	5

The list contains all possible ways in which 13 can be written as the sum of three counting numbers. The starred (*) combinations are the only ones that could be the sides of a triangle whose perimeter is 13. Why?
(<u>5</u> triangles)

There are 180 chips in a box. Each chip is marked with either an odd number or an even number. Some of the chips are red, some are white, and some are blue. There are 24 red even chips, 29 blue odd chips, 93 even chips, and 30 of the 64 white chips are even. How many of the chips in the box are red? blue even?

Carlota has 36 coins consisting of nickels, dimes, or quarters. Nineteen of her coins are not nickels, and all but 27 of her coins are quarters. How much money does she have?

There are 180 chips in a box. Each chip is marked with either an odd number or an even number. Some of the chips are red, some are white, and some are blue. There are 24 red even chips, 29 blue odd chips, 93 even chips, and 30 of the 64 white chips are even. How many of the chips in the box are red? (<u>48</u>)   blue even? (<u>39</u>)

<u>Strategy: Make a List</u>

	Odd	Even	Total
Red	24	24	48
White	34	30	64
Blue	29	39	68
Total	87	93	180

Carlota has 36 coins consisting of nickels, dimes, and quarters. Nineteen of her coins are not nickels, and all but 27 of her coins are quarters. How much money does she have?

<u>Strategy: Make a List</u>

There are 17 nickels. Why?
There are 10 dimes. Why?
Carlota has 17 nickels, 10 dimes, and 9 quarters.
The total value of the coins is <u>$4.10.</u>

I am thinking of 3 different whole numbers. The smallest is two more than half the largest, the average of the three numbers is 30, and one of the numbers is a perfect square. Find the numbers.

How many different ways can 11 pennies be put into three boxes so that each box ends up with an odd number of pennies?

I am thinking of 3 different whole numbers. The smallest is two more than half the largest, the average of the three numbers is 30, and one of the numbers is a perfect square. Find the numbers.

Strategies: Guess and Test Use a Variable Make a List

The sum of the three numbers must be 90. Why?
The largest number must be even. Why?

Smallest # $X/2 + 2$	Middle # Perfect Square	Largest # $X \leftarrow$ guess	
22	28	40	no
21	31	38	no
20	34	36	no
19	37	34	no
. . .			
23	25	42	yes

The numbers are 23, 25, and 42.

How many different ways can 11 pennies be put into three boxes so that each box ends up with an odd number of pennies?

Strategy: Make a List

A	B	C	# of ways	
1	1	9	3	(119, 191, 911)
1	3	7	6	
1	5	5	3	
3	3	5	3	

Total number of ways = 15

      PROBLEM SOLVING CHALLENGES

At the Apollo athletic banquet, every 2 guests shared a dish of meat, every 4 guests shared a dish of vegetables, and every 3 guests shared a dish of rice. How many guests were there if a total of 117 dishes were served at the banquet?

Darla has only dimes and quarters in her coin collection. She has 70 less quarters than dimes and one-ninth of her coins are quarters. What is the total value of her coin collection?

At the Apollo athletic banquet, every 2 guests shared a dish of meat, every 4 guests shared a dish of vegetables, and every 3 guests shared a dish of rice. How many guests were there if a total of 117 dishes were served at the banquet?

Solution I Strategies: Guess and Test Make a List
Note that the number of guests must be a multiple of 12. Why?

# of guests	# meat dishes	# veg. dishes	# rice dishes	# of dishes	
24	12	6	8	26	no
120	60	30	40	130	no
		. . .			
108	54	27	36	117	yes

108 guests were served at the banquet.

Solution II Strategy: Use a Variable
Let G = number of guests. Then G/2 + G/4 + G/3 = 117.
Hence, (13/12)G = 117 and G = 108.
Therefore, 108 guests were served at the banquet.

Darla has only dimes and quarters in her coin collection. She has 70 less quarters than dimes and one-ninth of her coins are quarters. What is the total value of her coin collection?

Strategy: Draw a Diagram

Each square must contain 10 coins. Why?
Hence, the total value of the coins is $10.50. Why?

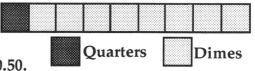

Quarters   Dimes

Strategy: Use a Variable

Let Q = number of quarters and let D = number of dimes.
Then Q = (D + Q)/9 and D = Q + 70.
This means that Darla has 10 quarters and 80 dimes.
Hence, the total value of the coins is $10.50.

   PROBLEM SOLVING CHALLENGES

What is the remainder when 3^{99} is divided by:
a. 4?   b. 5?   c. 7?

Lonnie and Amber bought identical boxes of stationery. Amber used hers to write one-sheet letters and Lonnie used hers to write two-sheet letters. Lonnie used all her sheets and had six envelopes left over. Amber used all her envelopes and had fifteen sheets left over. How many envelopes were there in each box?

What is the remainder when 3^{99} is divided by: a. 4? b. 5? c. 7?

Strategy: Solve a Simpler Problem Make a List Look for a Pattern

	3^1	3^2	3^3	3^4	3^5	3^6	3^7	3^8	...	3^{99}
Rem (÷ 4)	3	1	3	1	3	1	3	1	...	<u>3</u>
Rem (÷ 5)	3	4	2	1	3	4	2	1	...	<u>2</u>
Rem (÷ 7)	3	2	6	4	5	1	3	2	...	<u>6</u>

Lonnie and Amber bought identical boxes of stationery. Amber used hers to write one-sheet letters and Lonnie used hers to write two-sheet letters. Lonnie used all her sheets and had six envelopes left over. Amber used all her envelopes and had fifteen sheets left over. How many envelopes were there in each box?

Solution I Strategy: Guess and Test

Amber: The number of sheets is 15 more than the number of envelopes.
Lonnie: The number of envelopes is 6 more than half the number of sheets.

# of Envelopes (E)	# of Sheets (S)	E = 6 + 1/2 of S	
45	60	45 = 6 + 30	No
35	50	35 = 6 + 25	No
27	42	27 = 6 + 21	Yes

There were <u>27 envelopes</u> in each box.

Solution II Strategy: Use a Variable

Let S = # of sheets and E = # of envelopes in a box.
Lonnie: Wrote S/2 letters and used S/2 envelopes. Therefore, E - S/2 = 6.
Amber: Wrote S letters and used E envelopes. Therefore, S - E = 15.
Hence, S = 42 and E = 27. There were <u>27 envelopes</u> in each box.

PROBLEM SOLVING CHALLENGES

There are between 300 and 350 books on a shelf. Forty percent of the books are textbooks and one-ninth are workbooks. How many books on the shelf are neither textbooks nor workbooks?

A fireman is standing on the middle rung of a ladder. When the smoke cleared somewhat, he moved 7 rungs up the ladder. Later, when the smoke got worse, he stepped down 11 rungs. Finally, after after the smoke cleared, he went up 17 steps to the top rung. How many rungs are in the ladder?

There are between 300 and 350 books on a shelf. Forty percent of the books are textbooks and one-ninth are workbooks. How many books on the shelf are neither textbooks nor workbooks?

Strategy: Make a List

40% = 2/5   2/5 + 1/9 = 23/45
Therefore, the number of books is a multiple of 45. Why?
Multiples of 45:   45 90 135 180 225 270 315 360 405 ...
There are 315 books on the shelf. Why?
Hence, <u>154 books</u> are neither textbooks nor workbooks. (22/45 x 315 = 154)

A fireman is standing on the middle rung of a ladder. When the smoke cleared somewhat, he moved 7 rungs up the ladder. Later, when the smoke got worse, he stepped down 11 rungs. Finally, after after the smoke cleared, he went up 17 steps to the top rung. How many rungs are in the ladder?

Solution I Strategy: Draw a Diagram

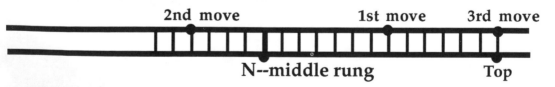

If the Nth rung is the middle rung, the fireman must move 7-11+17 = 13 rungs to get to the top rung. Verify.   13 rungs + 1 rung + 13 rungs = 27 rungs
There are <u>27 rungs</u> in the ladder.

Solution II Strategy: Use a Variable

Let R = number of rungs on ladder.
Then (R+1)/2 + 7 - 11 + 17 = R. Why?
Thus, R = 27. There are <u>27 rungs</u> in the ladder.

           PROBLEM SOLVING CHALLENGES

The Suds soap company surveyed some people to determine whether they use the liquid or the powder form of a certain brand of soap. Use the below clues to find the total number of people interviewed:
* 2/5 use the liquid
* 1/3 use the powder
* 1/7 use both the liquid and the powder
* 258 use neither the liquid nor the powder.

Gary weighs 44 pounds plus half his weight, and Gary's sister Karen weighs 30 pounds plus one-third her weight. Which of the following is their total weight in pounds?

91   96   128   133   168

The Suds soap company surveyed some people to determine whether they use the liquid or the powder form of a certain brand of soap. Use the below clues to find the total number of people interviewed.
* 2/5 use the liquid   * 1/3 use the powder
* 1/7 use both the liquid and the powder
* 258 use neither the liquid nor the powder.

Strategy: Draw a Diagram

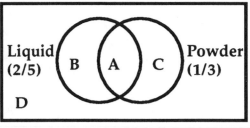

Let N = number of people interviewed.
There are 4 distinct regions
(A, B, C, D) in the Venn diagram.
Region A: (1/7)N
Region B: (2/5 - 1/7)N = 9/35 N
Region C: (1/3 - 1/7)N = 4/21 N
Region D: 1 - 1/7 N - 9/35 N - 4/21 N = 43/105 N
Therefore, 43/105 N = 258. Thus, N = 630.   <u>630</u> people were interviewed.

Gary weighs 44 pounds plus half his weight, and Gary's sister Karen weighs 30 pounds plus one-third her weight. Which of the following is their total weight in pounds?
     91   96   128   133   168

Solution I Strategy: Guess and Test

Gary		Karen	
Weight	1/2 of weight + 44	Weight	1/3 of weight + 30
100	50+44=94	60	20+30=50
90	45+44=89	54	18+30=48
88	44+44=88	45	15+30=45

Gary's weight is 88 pounds and Karen's weight is 45 pounds.
Total weight is <u>133 pounds</u>.

Solution II Strategy: Use a Variable

Let G = Gary's weight in pounds. Then $44 + 1/2G = G \Rightarrow G = 88$.
Let K = Karen's weight in pounds. Then $30 + 1/3K = K \Rightarrow K = 45$.
Total weight = 88 + 45 = <u>133 pounds</u>.

              PROBLEM SOLVING CHALLENGES

How many different ways can ten dimes be placed into three boxes so that each box ends up with at least 20 cents?

There are two piles of chips with 5 chips in each pile. Two players take turns removing either one chip from one of the piles or one chip from each of the two piles. The winner is the player that removes the last chip. Find a strategy that will make the first player a sure winner.

Problem Solving (14)

How many different ways can ten dimes be placed into three boxes so that each box ends up with at least 20 cents?

Solution I Strategy: Make a List

Number of Dimes

BOX A	2	2	6	2	2	3	3	5	5	2	4	4	3	3	4
BOX B	2	6	2	3	5	5	2	3	2	4	2	4	3	4	3
BOX C	6	2	2	5	3	2	5	2	3	4	4	2	4	3	3

There are <u>15 ways</u> to place the dimes.

Solution II Strategy: Solve a Simpler Problem

Each box must contain at least 2 dimes for a total of at least 6 dimes.

# of dimes	6	7	8	9	10
# of ways	1	3	6	10	<u>15</u>

Extension: Solve the problem if there are:

15 dimes (<u>78 ways</u>)   65 dimes (<u>1830</u> = 1+2+3+ . . . +60)

There are two piles of chips with 5 chips in each pile. Two players take turns removing either one chip from one of the piles or one chip from each of the two piles. The winner is the player that removes the last chip. Find a strategy that will make the first player a sure winner.

Strategy: Use a Model

The first player should remove 1 chip from each pile on the first move. For each subsequent move, the first player should make selections that are identical to those made by the second player.

              PROBLEM SOLVING CHALLENGES

The time now is between 4:00 p.m. and 5:00 p.m. In 46 more minutes, it will be as many minutes before 6:00 p.m. as it was after 4:00 p.m. a half hour ago. What is the time now?

On a 25-question test, a student gets 4 points for each correct answer and loses 2 points for each incorrect answer. Jim answered every question on the test and scored 64 points. How many questions did he answer correctly?

The time now is between 4:00 p.m. and 5:00 p.m. In 46 more minutes, it will be as many minutes before 6:00 p.m. as it was after 4:00 p.m. a half hour ago. What is the time now?

Solution I Strategy: Guess and Test

Time (p.m.)	Now	30 min. ago	46 min. from now	
Guess →	5:00	4:30	5:46	no
	4:40	4:10	5:26	no
	. . .			
	4:52	4:22	5:38	yes

Solution II Strategies: Draw a Diagram Use a Variable

From the diagram, X - 30 = 120 - (X + 46). Why?
Hence, X = 52.   The time now is 4:52 p.m.

On a 25-question test, a student gets 4 points for each correct answer and loses 2 points for each incorrect answer. Jim answered every question on the test and scored 64 points. How many questions did he answer correctly?

Solution I Strategy: Guess and Test

# correct	# incorrect	Score	
24	1	94	(96-2)
22	3	82	(88-6)
. . .			
19	6	64	(76-12)

Solution II Strategy: Use a Variable

Let C = number of correct answers. Then 25 - C = number of incorrect answers. Kevin received 4C points for the correct answers and lost 2(25 - C) points for the incorrect answers. Thus, 4C - 2(25 - C) = 64 $\Rightarrow$ C = 19.
Jim answered 19 questions correctly.

Use the below clues to help you determine the number of nickels that are in a pile of coins containing only nickels, dimes, and quarters:

*The number of dimes is five more than the number of nickels.

*Twelve of the coins are not dimes.

*The total value of the coins is $2.80.

Complete the following sequence so that after the first two terms, each successive term is the average of all the preceding terms.

13   —   —   22   —   —

Problem Solving (16)

Use the below clues to help you determine the number of nickels that are in a pile of coins containing only nickels, dimes, and quarters:

*The number of dimes is five more than the number of nickels.

*Twelve of the coins are not dimes.

*The total value of the coins is $2.80.

Solution I Strategies: Guess and Test Make a List

Nickels	Dimes	Quarters	Value	
Guess → 5	10	7	25+100+175=$3.00	No
6	11	6	30+110+150=$2.90	No
7	12	5	35+120+125=$2.80	YES
8	13	4	40+130+100=$2.70	No

There are 7 nickels in the pile.

Solution II Strategy: Use a Variable

Let X = # of nickels. Then # of dimes = X + 5 and # of quarters = 12 - X.

Hence, 5X + 10(X + 5) + 25(12 - X) = 280. Why?

Therefore, X = 7. Verify. There are 7 nickels in the pile.

Complete the following sequence so that after the first two terms, each successive term is the average of all the preceding terms.

$$13 \quad \text{—} \quad \text{—} \quad 22 \quad \text{—} \quad \text{—}$$

Strategy: Use a Variable

$$13 \quad \underset{X}{\text{—}} \quad \underset{(13+X)/2}{\text{—}} \quad 22 \quad \text{—} \quad \text{—}$$

[13 + X + (13 + X)/2]/3 = 22. Why?

Therefore, X = 31. Every term after the 2nd term is 22. Why?

$$13 \quad \underline{31} \quad \underline{22} \quad 22 \quad \underline{22} \quad \underline{22}$$

       PROBLEM SOLVING CHALLENGES

There are 65 diplomats seated at a round table. Each shakes hands with the person to the right and left. How many handshakes were there?

There were twice as many children as adults at a family reunion. Every adult shook hands once with all the other adults. Also, every child shook hands once with all the other children. How many people were at the reunion given that the total number of handshakes was 81?

There are 65 diplomats seated at a round table. Each shakes hands with the person to the right and left. How many handshakes were there?

Strategies: Solve a Simpler Problem   Make a List

# of diplomats	3	4	5	6	...	N
# of handshakes	3	4	5	6	...	?

The pattern suggests that for 65 diplomats, there were <u>65</u> handshakes.

AB BC CD DA
BA CB DC AD
4 handshakes only

There were twice as many children as adults at a family reunion. Every adult shook hands once with all the other adults. Also, every child shook hands once with all the other children. How many people were at the reunion given that the total number of handshakes was 81?

Strategies: Solve a Simpler Problem   Make a List

# of people	2	3	4	5	6	7	8	9	10	11	12
# of handshakes	1	3	6	10	15	21	28	36	45	55	66

There were 6 adults (15 handshakes) and 12 children (66 handshakes). Thus, there were <u>18 people</u> at the reunion.

A Lake City club that wants stop lights at a crossroads intersection decided to distribute a petition asking for signatures of residents favoring their position. Each day during the month of April, they got 2 more signatures than the previous day. The total number of signatures they got during the first 18 days was the same as the total for the other days. How many people signed the petition in April?

In a group of 90 college students, 34 are men, 22 are seniors, and 36 are neither seniors nor juniors. Of the women in the group, 26 are juniors and 9 are seniors. How many men in the group are not juniors?

A Lake City club that wants stop lights at a crossroads intersection decided to distribute a petition asking for signatures of residents favoring their position. Each day during the month of April, they got 2 more signatures than the previous day. The total number of signatures they got during the first 18 days was the same as the total for the other days. How many people signed the petition in April?

Strategy: Use a Variable

Day:	1	2	3	...	18	19	20	...	30
# signatures:	s	s+2	s+4	...	s+34	s+36	s+38	...	s+58

$$\text{Sum} = 18s + 306 \qquad \text{Sum} = 12s + 564$$

$$18s + 306 = 12s + 564 \Rightarrow s = 43.$$

Total number of signatures = $(18s + 306) + (12s + 564) = 30s + 870 = \underline{2160}$.

In a group of 90 college students, 34 are men, 22 are seniors, and 36 are neither seniors nor juniors. Of the women in the group, 26 are juniors and 9 are seniors. How many men in the group are not juniors?   ($\underline{28}$ = 13 + 15)

Strategy: Make a List

	Jr.	Sr.	Other	Total
M	6	13	15	34
W	26	9	21	56
Total	32	22	36	90

          PROBLEM SOLVING CHALLENGES

A 20-inch by 32-inch rectangular sheet of cardboard is made into an open top box by first cutting identical squares from each corner and then folding up the sides. What is the largest possible volume of the box given that each edge of the cut out square is a whole number?

How many different ways are there to get to the top of a nine-step stairway if you take either one or two steps at a time?

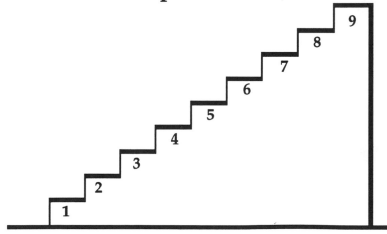

A 20-inch by 32-inch rectangular sheet of cardboard is made into an open top box by first cutting identical squares from each corner and then folding up the sides. What is the largest possible volume of the box given that each edge of the cut out square is a whole number?

Strategies: Draw a Diagram   Guess and Test

Height of box = side of removed square.

Height	Width	Length	Volume
1	18	30	540
2	16	28	896
3	14	26	1092
4	12	24	1152
5	10	22	1100
6	8	20	960

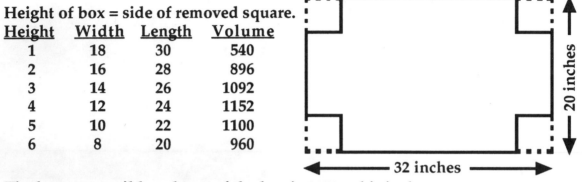

The largest possible volume of the box is <u>1152 cubic inches</u>.

Alternate Strategy: Use a Variable

How many different ways are there to get to the top of a nine-step stairway if you take either one or two steps at a time?

Strategies: Draw a Diagram   Make a List   Look for a Pattern

To Step	# of ways
1	1
2	2
3	3
4	5
5	8
6	13
.	.
.	.
.	.

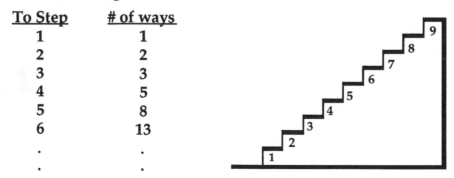

The pattern suggests that there are <u>55 ways</u> to get to step 9. Verify.

          PROBLEM SOLVING CHALLENGES

Find the 500th digit after the decimal point in each of the following:

a. $0.\overline{3861}$ b. $0.\overline{285714}$ c. $0.\overline{13689523}$

Note: $0.\overline{273} = 0.273273273273 \ldots$

A bookstore bought 100 books for $100. The manager paid three different prices: $10.00, $3.00, and $0.50. If she bought at least one of each type of book, how many books were purchased at each price?

Find the 500th digit after the decimal point in each of the following:

a. $0.\overline{3861}$ b. $0.\overline{285714}$ c. $0.\overline{13689523}$

Note: $0.\overline{273} = 0.273273273273 \ldots$

Strategies: Make a List Look for a Pattern

a. $0.\overline{3861}$ Every 4th digit is 1 $\Rightarrow$ 500th digit is <u>1</u>.

b. $0.\overline{285714}$ Every 6th digit is 4 $\Rightarrow$ 500th digit is <u>8</u>.

c. $0.\overline{13689523}$ The 500th digit is <u>5</u>. Why?

A bookstore bought 100 books for $100. The manager paid three different prices: $10.00, $3.00, and $0.50. If she bought at least one of each type of book, how many books were purchased at each price?

Strategy: Guess and Test

The number of $0.50 books must be an even number. Why?
The number of $10 books must be less than 10. Why?

# of $10 books	# of $3 books	# of $.5 books	
8 ($80)	2 ($6)	90 ($45.00)	No (>$100)
7 ($70)	1 ($3)	92 ($46.00)	No (>$100)
6 ($60)	2 ($6)	92 ($46.00)	No (>$100)
5 ($50)	1 ($3)	94 ($47.00)	YES (=$100)

The manager bought <u>5 books at $10, 1 book at $3, and 94 books at $0.50</u>.

            PROBLEM SOLVING CHALLENGES

The distance between each of the posts in a fence along a property line is 3.5 meters. It is 231 meters from the fifth post to the last one. How many posts are in the fence?

The Discovery School pep club is 5/8 girls. After 14 more boys joined the club, the number of girls was exactly the same as the number of boys. How many girls belong to the club?

The distance between each of the posts in a fence along a property line is 3.5 meters. It is 231 meters from the fifth post to the last one. How many posts are in the fence?

Strategies: Draw a Diagram   Solve a Simpler Problem

5   6   7   8   N
◀———————— 231 meters ————————▶

There are sixty-six 3.5-meter long sections between the 5th post and the last post. Why? Hence, the total number of posts is 66 + 1 + 4 = <u>71</u>.

The Discovery School pep club is 5/8 girls. After 14 more boys joined the club, the number of girls was exactly the same as the number of boys. How many girls belong to the club?

Solution I Strategy: Guess and Test
The original number (N) of students is a multiple of 8. Why?

Original # (N)	24	32	40	48	56
G = 5/8 of N	15	20	25	30	35
B = N - G	9	12	15	18	21
Is B + 14 = G?	no	no	no	no	YES

There are 5/8 of 56 = <u>35 girls</u> in the club.

Solution II Strategy: Draw a Diagram

Let ☐ represent 1/8 the previous number of students in the club.
Before ▭▭▭▭▭|▭▭▭   After ▭▭▭▭▭|▭▭▭
     Girls   Boys   Girls   Boys
Why does ▭▭ represent 14 students? Explain why there are now 70 students in the club. There are <u>35 girls</u> in the club.

Solution III Strategy: Use a Variable
Let N represent the original number of students in the club. The number of girls = 5/8 of N. New number of students = N + 14. There are (N + 14)/2 boys in the club. Why is 5/8 of N = (N + 14)/2? Therefore, N = 56.
Hence, <u>the number of girls = 35</u>.

     PROBLEM SOLVING CHALLENGES

How many beads are hidden under the cloud?

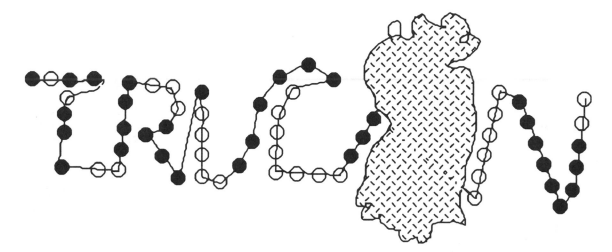

Suppose the below circles have radii 10 units, 6 units, and 4 units, respectively. What is the difference between the shaded area inside the big circle and the shaded area outside the big circle?

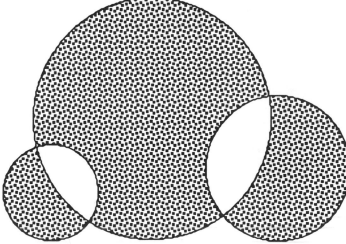

How many beads are hidden under the cloud?

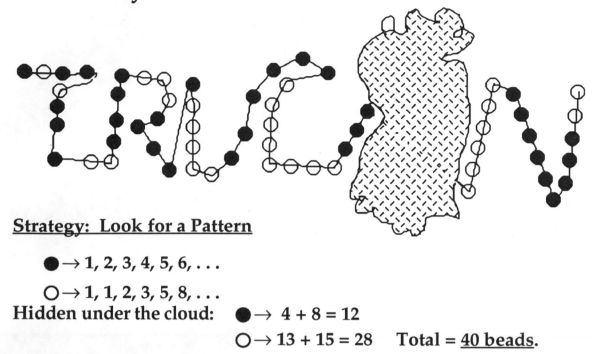

Strategy: Look for a Pattern

● → 1, 2, 3, 4, 5, 6, . . .

○ → 1, 1, 2, 3, 5, 8, . . .

Hidden under the cloud: ● → 4 + 8 = 12

                         ○ → 13 + 15 = 28   Total = <u>40 beads</u>.

Suppose the below circles have radii 10 units, 6 units, and 4 units, respectively. What is the difference between the shaded area inside the big circle and the shaded area outside the big circle?

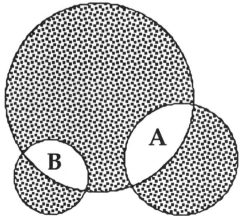

Area of largest circle = 100π.

Area of larger circle = 36π.

Area of smallest circle = 16π.

Area inside largest circle = $100\pi - A - B$.

Area outside largest circle
= $(36\pi - A) + (16\pi - B)$.

Difference in area
= $(100\pi - A - B) - (36\pi - A) - (16\pi - B) = \underline{48\pi}$.

     PROBLEM SOLVING CHALLENGES

Find the perimeter and the area of the figure that is formed by connecting consecutive midpoints of a rectangle which has width **24** inches and length **32** inches.

Beth has **30** white chips and **30** black chips. She used **35** of these chips to form a rectangular arrangement with **20** white chips on the edges and **15** inner black chips.

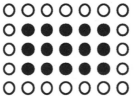

Using some of the **30** white chips and some of the **30** black chips, show how Beth can make a rectangular arrangement where the number of white chips on the edges is the same as the number of inner black chips.

Find the perimeter and the area of the figure that is formed by connecting consecutive midpoints of a rectangle which has width 24 inches and length 32 inches.

Strategy: Draw a Diagram

In the diagram, $MN^2 = 12^2 + 16^2$ (Pythagorean Theorem)
Therefore, MN = 20 inches.
Why is NP = PQ = QM = MN?
Perimeter of MNPQ = 20 x 4 = __80 inches__

Area of shaded region
= area of ABCD - 4x area of triangle NAM. Why?
= 32 x 24 - 4 x 1/2 x 12 x 16 = __384 square inches__.

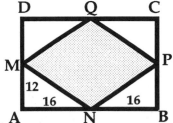

Beth has 30 white chips and 30 black chips. She used 35 of these chips to form a rectangular arrangement with 20 white chips on the edges and 15 inner black chips.

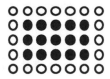

Using some of the 30 white chips and some of the 30 black chips, show how Beth can make a rectangular arrangement where the number of white chips on the edges is the same as the number of inner black chips.

Strategies: Use a Model Guess and Test Draw a Diagram

Beth can form an __8x6__ rectangular arrangement as shown.
There are 24 white chips and 24 black chips.

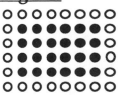

     PROBLEM SOLVING CHALLENGES

Select a number. Write that number above A and above B. Find the numbers C through I by adding the preceding two numbers. The sum of all the numbers (A-I) should be 11 times the number above F. Verify.

___ ___ ___ ___ ___ ___ ___ ___ ___
A   B   C   D   E   F   G   H   I

Show why 11 x F is always equal to A+B+C+...+I.

In the figure below, suppose each rectangle has width 4 cm and perimeter 28 cm. Find the distance around the figure.

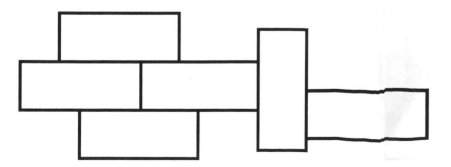

Select a number. Write that number above A and above B. Find the numbers C through I by adding the preceding two numbers. The sum of all the numbers (A-I) should be 11 times the number above F. Verify.

N	N	$2N$	$3N$	$5N$	$8N$	$13N$	$21N$	$34N$
A	**B**	**C**	**D**	**E**	**F**	**G**	**H**	**I**

Show why 11 x F is always equal to A+B+C+...+I.

Strategy: Use a Variable

Let N be the number above A and above B.
Sum of numbers (A-I) = (1+1+2+3+5+8+13+21+34)N = 88N = 11(8N) = 11 x F.

In the figure below, suppose each rectangle has width 4 cm and perimeter 28 cm. Find the distance around the figure.

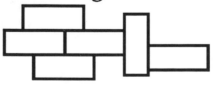

Strategy: Use a Model
Each rectangle has a length of 10 cm.
The total horizontal length of the figure is 68 cm (2 x 34). Verify.
The total vertical length is 36 cm (5x4 + 6 + 10).
The distance around the figure = 104 cm.

Extension: What is the distance around the figure given that each rectangle has width W and length L? (8L + 6W)

	1	**2**	**3**	**4**	**5**	
1	25	30	35	40	45	· · ·
2	30	35	40	45	50	· · ·
3	35	40	45	50	55	· · ·
4	40	45	50	55	60	· · ·

Find the missing numbers suggested by the above patterns. The first two are done for you.

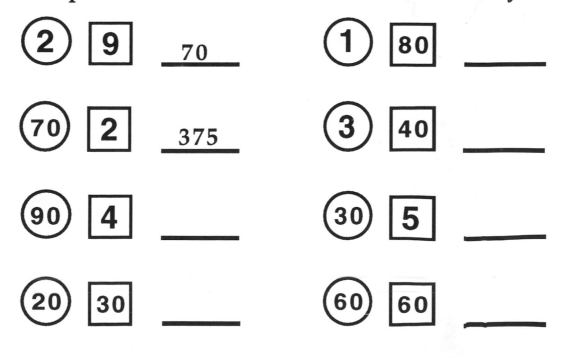

(2) [9]   70   (1) [80] ____

(70) [2]   375   (3) [40] ____

(90) [4] ____   (30) [5] ____

(20) [30] ____   (60) [60] ____

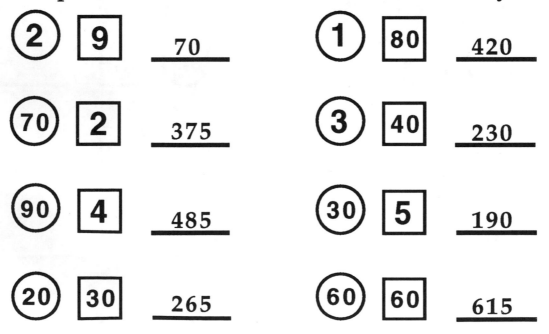

	1	**2**	**3**	**4**	**5**	
1	25	30	35	40	45	· · ·
2	30	35	40	45	50	· · ·
3	35	40	45	50	55	· · ·
4	40	45	50	55	60	· · ·

Find the missing numbers suggested by the above patterns. The first two are done for you.

② ⑨	__70__	① 80	__420__
⑦⓪ ②	__375__	③ 40	__230__
⑨⓪ 4	__485__	③⓪ 5	__190__
②⓪ 30	__265__	⑥⓪ 60	__615__

     PROBLEM SOLVING CHALLENGES